Facing the Monster

Facing the MONSTER

How One Person
Can Fight
Child Slavery

CAROL HART METZKER

OPEN BOOK
EDITIONS
A Berrett–Koehler Partner

Facing the Monster
How One Person Can Fight Child Slavery

iUniverse books may be ordered through booksellers or by contacting:

iUniverse
1663 Liberty Drive
Bloomington, IN 47403
www.iuniverse.com
1-800-Authors (1-800-288-4677)

Because of the dynamic nature of the Internet, any web addresses or links contained in this book may have changed since publication and may no longer be valid. The views expressed in this work are solely those of the author and do not necessarily reflect the views of the publisher, and the publisher hereby disclaims any responsibility for them.

Front cover photograph: A girl crying, painted by survivors of child slavery on a wall at Punarnawa Ashram. Photographed and used by permission of Punarnawa Ashram. Photograph ©2011 by Carol Hart Metzker.

Note: In this book, names of many survivors have been changed to safeguard their identity. This is done for their privacy and protection. Name changes are noted with an asterisk (*).

ISBN: 978-1-4759-3108-2 (sc)
ISBN: 978-1-4759-3107-5 (hc)
ISBN: 978-1-4759-3109-9 (e)

Library of Congress Control Number: 2012909886

Printed in the United States of America

iUniverse rev. date: 06/14/2012

This book is dedicated to children who
courageously survive victimization.

It also honors the readers who enter the survivors'
world through these pages, emerge better
informed, and take a stand to help them.

Contents

Part III: Taking Action, Making Change

Preface

When I began work as a professional writer in 2001, I would never have guessed that child slavery, human trafficking, and exploitation would become subjects of my articles or a book. My newly minted master's degree in social and organizational learning from George Mason University was about how people work and interact together. My print and online stories focused on successful global corporations and nimble entrepreneurs, psychology behind innovation in business, human interaction, and communication in a big, messy, complicated, connected system we call the world.

Yet it was precisely the curiosity of a writer that accidentally led me to the dark, hidden side of those same stories. Unknown to me at graduation, my degree also encompassed what I needed in order to expand my horizons beyond overt, positive stories and practices, and to face the evil ones. It didn't take too many probing questions about how certain companies generated so much profit, or how certain jobs were accomplished or needs were fulfilled in a global society, to figure out that something is dreadfully wrong, that it needs to be fixed, and that it *can* be changed.

A trip to India in 2004 landed me at a rehabilitation center for children rescued from slavery. My need for truth about modern slavery and ways to solve it sparked interaction and interviews with rescued slaves, crime victims, and compassionate souls who rescue victims and help survivors. My path to answers, as well as the answers themselves, became the primary research that informed this book.

The truth is clear. Woven into the very fabric of our daily lives and work is modern slavery. It is an issue—an invisible beast—that touches every aspect of our world—economics, morality, psychology, business, art, justice, and everything else. A quick visit to www.slaveryfootprint.org points to our undeniable role in perpetuating the carefully hidden crimes of slaveholders: our children play with slave-produced soccer balls, women wear cosmetics made with sparkly mica mined by child slaves, and we consume food and beverages produced by workers who are unpaid, unable to leave, and held by violence or threats. Who wouldn't look for a fair trade symbol on a package of tea, befriend a child at risk, or ask an elected official to look at laws that protect people, in order to ensure everyone's liberty? We just need to know to take those actions.

This book was written not just to dig up dirt, but also to help solve a problem! Because modern slavery touches every aspect of our lives, it can be addressed and solved from every point. Each person has a special gift, and that gift can be applied to abolishing child slavery. I hope that the following pages that share my journey into a dark, secret world will help you understand why your help is needed. I hope that you, as a conscience-driven individual, will adopt the simple solutions—all accomplished without leaving the country or giving a fortune—outlined at the end of the book as your next steps. I hope that you, too, will feel the hope and inspiration of the stories of resilient children and unassuming heroes and choose to face and fight the monster of child slavery.

Note: In this book, names of many survivors have been changed to safeguard their identity. This is done for their privacy and protection. Name changes are noted with an asterisk (*).

Acknowledgments

Riding the elevator down and into the underworld of slavery would have been impossible without the support of generous family and friends—brilliant lamps in the darkness. There were many challenges to navigate: sensitively writing the stories of child slaves and accurately portraying other people's experiences; revealing my personal, private emotions and vulnerabilities; and determining how best to help readers understand what is happening today without overwhelming them. The light of my caring companions served as beacons.

Deep gratitude goes to the people who trusted me with their stories. Rescued slaves, liberators, abolitionists, staff members of Free the Slaves, as well as residents and team members of Dawn's Place, Mukti Ashram, Balika Ashram, Bal Vikas Ashram, and Punarnawa Ashram. Kevin, Ginny, Supriya, Rajneesh, Michelle, Eileen, Ron, Mark L., Bob, Mark R., Ceal, and others graciously gave their time to talk with me about their experiences.

Accolades go to Rotarians who didn't shy away from trips to places that were atypical destinations for tourists. Many fellow travelers, who didn't enjoy the step off tourism's marble staircase into the dirt pit of reality, kindly let go of grudges. Of particular note, thanks to Dave Ellis, whose support never waned over the years; to Vasanth Prabhu, a miracle worker in many countries; and to Mike Korengel, who braved two crazy trips to India and found that "lightning *could* strike twice in the same place!"

Sincere appreciation extends to the Circle of Friends, including Connie, Carol, Gina, Marie, and Ann for sharing this journey.

Thank you to members of the Rotary Club of West Chester Downtown for your willingness to become part of this ongoing story. Phoebe, Clint, Anita, Randy, Annalie, Dennis, Eric, Dom, Eric, Lance, Merry, Marie, Joyce, Bob, Lizabeth, Chris, and others live Rotary's motto: "Service above Self." Thanks also to other Rotarians—Bruce, Glen, Bronwyn, Bonnie, and others—whose help with books and other projects for survivors has been invaluable.

Many trusted readers and friends offered comments and feedback that made the manuscript better. Annette Evans helped me focus, understand the book's purpose, and talked late into the night about revealing vulnerability in writing and facing monsters. Bob Frye, Elizabeth Killough, Ann Upton, Mark Little, Noah Blumenthal, Victoria Dow, Annalie Korengel Lorgus, Ginny Baumann, Michelle, and others provided perspective and suggestions. Thank you to Laura Bernstein for helping to put a pen in my hand years ago.

Appreciation goes to numerous abolitionists, fair trade advocates, members of Willistown Friends Meeting, and participants of Dress for a Good Cause.

I am indebted to Mark Little, whose courageous actions got this project started and whose faithful heart keeps it going.

To my great lights in life—Elizabeth, Kathryn, and Eric—there are not enough words to capture my sentiments about their extraordinary contributions to the manuscript and to the underlying journey. Sincere thanks to Elizabeth—profound soul, gentle friend, and patient teacher of quilting and character. Kudos to Kathryn—adventurous spirit, ultimate traveling companion in a developing nation, and good-natured adviser. Thank you to Eric—*anam cara*, humorist during my frustration, warrior during fear, and rock during uncertainty—for believing in me and our path every step of the way.

Prologue—Ceal and Jake, 1991

"You try now, Jake," Ceal gently encouraged her son.

The little dark-haired boy thrust his legs forward and then pulled them back. He hadn't fully gotten the knack of leaning forward and backward with the timing of the swing, so Ceal gave a gentle push every few motions of the pendulum.

"He's starting to get the hang of it," she told me. "The doctor says he has some catching up to do, but he's doing well. It's hard to say whether he's small because of a lack of nutrition or because his parents were small. We don't have any information about what his life was like before he lived at the orphanage."

Ceal and I talked quietly as we pushed our children on the swings. The chains that connected the faded, hard-rubber swing seats to the old-fashioned metal frame rubbed against large hooks. They created a rhythmic squeak: away and back, away and back. In the warm, whispering breeze, leaves on old, tall trees fluttered, forming ever-changing patterns of pale yellow sunlight and shadows across our faces.

We were the only parents in the little play area behind our eighteenth-century Quaker meetinghouse, where the rest of our congregation worshipped in silence. Ceal and I had left the hushed, centered service when the children in our laps became restless. Before their noise and physical activity could shift the tone of the meeting, we slipped out the back door of the simple fieldstone building. We ran across the green grass to a long, metal sliding board, a swing set, and a slightly rusty hand pump that drew cool drinking water. Our children—my Elizabeth at two years and Ceal's five-year-old Jake—were now quiet. Perhaps they were mesmerized by the rocking motion and rhythmic sounds of the swings. Maybe they were just deep and content in their childhood thoughts in the idyllic surroundings.

"Push me again now, Mom?" Jake asked Ceal.

"Jake's English is getting pretty good now too," I commented.

She nodded. "Sometimes he even tells us about his life in the orphanage in India before we adopted him," she said. She paused and turned toward me with serious eyes. "One night when I was reading him a bedtime story, he told me that the other children told him that Pete and I were slaveholders. That we had come to get him and that he would become our slave in America. That other Americans came and took other children from the Indian orphanage to be slaves."

"What on earth did you say to him after that?" I felt bewildered and disturbed. What an odd and frightening thing for children to say to such a tiny boy. Growing up, my cousins had warned me about the boogeyman, and children in my neighborhood swapped scary stories of fictional creatures that could kidnap and eat us. But the monsters were so ridiculous they were easily dismissed. I had never heard anything quite like this.

Ceal answered, "I told him we were not slaveholders. We were here to love him and care for him."

"Where do children get these sorts of ideas?" I asked. More carefully, cautiously, I inquired, "You don't think there could be any truth to their story about slavery, do you?"

"I don't know," Ceal said simply. And we left it at that.

That topic lay dormant for ten years. Had I listened more intently I might have noticed it returning. Like a mosquito flying ever closer to my ear, a distant hum grew stronger until it became a loud, annoying buzz. The sound announced the arrival of a menace—an encounter that could not be avoided. Now at close range, I had to face a real, roaring monster; we all would have to confront it because we could no longer deny the existence of the growing beast.

Part I:

Disturbing Discoveries: Modern Slavery

Chapter 1—Three Questions

At parties, sometimes I consider lying. Usually, evasion seems a better way to go. The truth about my travels to India and pastimes when at home can be awkward small talk at best and shocking table conversation at worst. When I end up in conversation with people whose conscience and curiosity enable candid, soulful interaction, however, three questions usually emerge about my quest and projects to help survivors of child slavery:

- What is the life of a child slave like?
- How does a rescue work?
- How can we help end slavery and aid survivors as they heal?

After nearly a decade of asking those same questions and seeking answers through books, trips to far-flung corners of the globe, and conversations with experts and survivors, I paint verbal pictures of Mahabala,* Supriya, and Asha.* Each of their stories—that of a boy who escaped slavery, a woman who participated in raids and rescues, and a girl who was learning to thrive in freedom—provide an answer to one of those commonly heard questions.

Mahabala had an irrepressible spirit. During a trip to a children's shelter in India, I felt his energy on the opposite side of our table. He seemed constantly in motion. Even when he was somewhat still he was making funny faces.

He was almost the shortest of his thirty-two new brothers, but he stuck out from the crowd because of his mischievous movements and expressions. When the taller boys lined up for a serious moment before mealtime, Mahabala the clown, with a green balloon hanging from his mouth, popped out from behind them. His dark brown eyes, nearly black hair cut very short, ears that slightly stuck out, and an impish grin that revealed teeth still growing in left me stifling laughter.

Running around the brick courtyard of his new home, his antics with bubbles gave no impression of his dark history. It was most likely his irrepressible spirit that had granted him a new existence. Mahabala had escaped slavery—ungodly hours of work at a hotel and beatings—on his own two feet. He ran away from a violent slaveholder and the hotel where he cleaned, served, and performed any task requested by patrons—for no pay. Mahabala had been a slave—not a sweatshop laborer, not a figure of speech—but a worker who was unpaid, unable to leave, and subjected to violence or threat of violence to himself or someone he loved.

Nowhere near adolescence, the little Indian orphan was given a second chance at life. Selfless, compassionate workers at this residential rehabilitation and education center and at other similar residential programs took care of Mahabala and youths like him: children who had survived human trafficking and slavery.

When I sat across the table from Mahabala, it was the end of 2010. Nearly one year to the day later, I had returned to India and was exploring another remote area of the country. There, my stockpile of stories—some horrifying and some hopeful—grew larger after traveling with Supriya, a director of an antislavery organization, and visiting an extraordinary campus where a girl named Asha was recovering.

Supriya told my traveling companions and me about her work as we rode in the back of a car and scooped scrumptious spicy noodles, using potato chips as spoons, from a big, shared box lunch. We were traveling in the poorest state in India, one whose poverty was nearly the intensity of sub-Saharan African nations. A toll collector in a booth along a rare, paved highway had just given us change in cookies because he had no cash. "Only here would that happen!" Supriya said, rolling with laughter.

Her tone became serious as she described a recent raid and rescue. Tension mounted as the slow bureaucratic process stretched on and on, like a rubber band seeking its limits. Starting at nine in the morning, she had spent several hours wading through red tape and a few more waiting for warrants. With each passing minute, odds increased that the timing and location of the secret raid would be leaked and the rescue would be foiled. If owners of the carpet factory and holders of the slaves who worked the looms were alerted, the slaves would be transferred to another location. They would be gone again.

Warrants finally secured, Supriya, police, and other government and nongovernment personnel entered a compound surrounded by seven-foot-high walls. In just minutes, they searched a large building but found no children, contrary to a tip-off deemed to be reliable. They ran to search the grounds. When they got to the very back of the compound, they found slaveholders hurling boys over the wall. Police who had rushed behind the property found additional slaveholders waiting to catch the boys as they were hurtled over the barrier.

Eleven boys were rescued, the small woman in blue jeans and sneakers informed us. Three had already been thrown bodily over the wall; eight were found before being tossed like objects. Eleven boys rescued—that was a good day's work.

It was Supriya who also led me to a newly established center for girls rescued from sex slavery. One day during our visit to the campus, I dashed back into the kitchen for a late morning cup of *chai* (tea). Asha, an older child, beckoned me to the screen-less open window. Her voice and face were animated, and I discovered the subject of her excitement. Across the back of her hand crept a bedraggled gray mouse with twitching nose and whiskers. Barely bigger than her knuckle, the mouse paused to take a bite of food she offered and then clutched the skin of her finger with its tiny front paws. When it made a dash for the windowsill and tried to scurry away, Asha gently scooped it back into her hand.

She had found the creature on the ground and rescued it from the prying eyes of the center's cat and dog. Her thrill over the mouse with matted fur and scrawny tail was complete, and she hovered over it like a new mother.

As I exited the kitchen, Asha put her hand close to my face, proudly displaying her new pet. It crawled a little too close for my comfort, and a mild screech and a burst of laughter flew from my mouth.

Finishing my chai in the garden, I wondered if Asha's affinity for the tiny gray mouse was based on her own past experiences.

Did she see a part of herself in the creature—once fearful and helpless against larger, more powerful animals and in need of rescue, food, and affection? What losses had she experienced during enslavement? Was she providing her mouse with the necessities she had once craved: home, sustenance, dignity, liberty, and assurance of life?

Later that day I encountered Asha again. She displayed a small cardboard box, the new home and bed of her adored mouse, and a smile that seemed to fill her whole face. The pleasure found in her pet—a creature to love, to nurture, and to call her own—was unmatched. Sometimes the smallest, humblest lives are light in a world of shadow.

Reflecting on her delight, I saw answers to how even one person can help survivors. Contributing the most basic provisions—food, a roof, care, a safe space where healing can happen and children can learn to live in freedom—are antidotes to the darkest evil on earth. We do not need to be the actual ones to cook the meal or give a hug—impractical solutions when survivors are recovering in faraway or secret locations; we simply need to support the caregivers who are already there. To prevent future victims we need to start taking steps to create a world in which we learn to pursue happiness without robbing anyone of liberty or life.

During my quest, each time I heard a story with a happy ending I breathed a sigh of relief. Each time I observed a survivor of slavery, my mind was deeply affected. Each experience during my journey created a new wrinkle of concern or laugh line of joy, a weight on my shoulders, or the lightening of my soul.

Mahabala, Supriya, and Asha left indelible marks on my mind; they helped shift my opinion about villains, heroes, and justice and expanded my knowledge about human rights and rehabilitation. My entire life had changed immeasurably, however, since 2004 when I met Mark, a world traveler and humanitarian, and Maina, a little girl whose shining eyes and smile had served as a beacon. They led me to an unexpected path, to the most unlikely vacation spot imaginable, and into a world of odd dreams, disturbing discoveries, and encounters with people whose voices had been silenced. They prodded me to seek solutions and to learn a thing or two about leadership. They also led me to a new understanding of human purpose and to new heights of insight, action, and hope.

Chapter 2—Mark and Maina, 2004

Walking to the front of a bus while bumping along back roads of India was no easy task. Big potholes in the hardened dirt and cracked concrete created a noisy, jolting ride that bounced our band of international travelers up and down and jostled us side to side. So we stayed in our seats.

Except for one. Hanging on to seatbacks, one man worked his way to the front of the bus. He began to address my fellow travelers and me, a group of tourists and volunteers who were spending a vacation visiting humanitarian projects between sightseeing jaunts—the magnificent Taj Mahal and a sublime bird sanctuary.

"Our visit today is to an *ashram*—a center, this one for children," he announced.

Not recalling the stop on our tour, I checked the itinerary. "Project visit" was all it stated. I shrugged, almost accustomed to the constant changes in schedules and seemingly complete disregard for appointment times that began the moment we arrived in Delhi. I supposed I would figure out where we were going and what we were doing when we got there, wherever "there" was.

Mark Little, the Englishman who valiantly made it to the front of the bus, described services for recovering children—medical and psychological treatment, education, vocational training, and returning home. I half-listened and jotted a few notes in my journal, distracted by exotic scenery outside the bus window: tropical plants, passing motorcycles that carried families of four, carts pulled by animals.

The road narrowed, eventually forcing the bus to stop. My fellow passengers and I disembarked on a lane that was now completely blocked by our behemoth bus. No matter, it seemed. By this time there were no other vehicles, not even a cart.

We walked the length of a long, tall wall, homing in on the sounds of children singing and clapping. We bent forward as we entered a campus through an open metal gate. Little girls decorated us with necklaces of marigolds and blessed us with red thumbprints of vermilion on our foreheads. Once adorned, we joined in a dance with the children.

Our laughing and smiling international band gathered with local humanitarian workers, teachers, and two teenage boys under a thatched-roof pavilion. A woman introduced the young men. "This is Huro, and this is Shivji," she said. "They lived here at the ashram for six months when they were younger."

Their harrowing experience began when six-year-old cousins Huro and Shivji were playing by a stream and a car pulled up beside them. A man got out and offered them candy, a rare treat for boys who lived in a desperately poor rural village. Huro and

Shivji accepted the sweets and the man's invitation for more. Deceived and whisked into the back of the car, the young boys were forced into the world of slavery.

Hundreds of miles from home Huro and Shivji were separated. Each was locked in a dark room with a carpet loom. Abused, given only a tiny amount of beans and rice, and provided with a tin cup for a toilet, each boy wove carpets for eighteen hours a day, never leaving his room.

From a village without modern communication, the uneducated, poverty-stricken parents were nearly helpless to find their sons. Without money, a car, or other resources they had no way to search for or publicize the loss of the boys. They were unable to fight corrupt officials who—in return for money—turned a blind eye to children's slave labor.

Never giving up hope, the parents appealed for help from local representatives of an international organization that rescued children in captivity. Five years later, humanitarian workers rescued Huro and Shivji, reunited them with their parents, and then brought them to the ashram to heal.

My half-listening was over. I scrawled notes in a tablet at a furious pace. My attention was now captive, my focus centered, every ounce of my brain's capacity fully tuned to the boys' story. I scribbled down the stages of recovery and the process of aiding a former child slave relearning to play and live in freedom. I scratched out notes about the significance of reading and writing—a marvelous game learned by children at the ashram and passed along to other children when they returned home—skills that help inoculate families against further enslavement. I observed Huro's deep-set eyes and dark expressions—he was now a young man studying to become a teacher.

A layer of dust and sweat from my hands coated my pen and camera. As the sun began to set, I slung my camera over my shoulder and strolled away from the group. I gazed at my surroundings. Boys played on monkey bars in front of a dormitory. Palms thrived around a low, concrete structure that held latrines. Huro and Shivji continued talking to members of our team under the thatched-roof gazebo. Away from the others, I allowed the scenery to absorb my thoughts ... until something in the corner of my eye caught my attention. Young girls in matching red-and-white-checked outfits, under the watchful eye of a motherly figure, stood in rows and watched my every movement.

I wandered over to them as though pulled gently by an invisible string. The woman—their teacher and caregiver—greeted me. She interpreted my hello for the girls and noticed that one of the smaller girls and I were looking at each other, smiling, connecting without saying a word.

"This is Maina," she said. Two weeks earlier, the eleven-year-old girl had been rescued from the circus, where she had been enslaved, the woman explained.

"Would she like to see a photo of herself?" I asked the teacher.

She translated. Maina's nod followed. I pulled the camera off my shoulder and held it to my eye. I snapped one last photo in the dimming daylight, and the automatic flash kicked into action. Before checking the photo myself, I turned the camera so Maina could see her image in the tiny screen. She grinned up at me as one of my fellow travelers nudged my elbow to herd me back to our bus.

It was there for a moment; its likeness was captured in pixels for eternity. Maina's beautiful smile, a result of her rescue and current safety, showed no trace of her previous trauma. It was illuminating. I rode the rays of her smile back to the ashram's gate.

Shock and disbelief, however, took hold as we retraced our steps down the lane. I began to shiver, and on the dark bus ride back to our quarters, I sobbed. Surely this experience was not real. Was it possible I had misunderstood? Could the ashram's sign, "No More Tools in Tiny Hands," be a prop, a trick, a fake? Where had Mark Little taken us? Did my history books lie or lead me astray by omission? Hadn't Quakers and other people of faith who conducted the American Underground Railroad—covert connections of escape routes and safe houses to help nineteenth-century slaves to freedom—ended this abomination?

How had such a dirty secret—a conspiracy of deceivers, thieves, sellers, buyers, users, abusers, and consumers—remained hidden from me for so long? My brain and heart searched for an answer that would bring peace and reassurance, but the truth remained solid and unwavering. Child slavery had never been abolished. It was alive and well. Human trafficking—a conduit for bringing people into slavery—slithered stealthily in shadow ... strong, powerful, and hungry for victims.

At my tenth consecutive hour of tears, I vowed that I would do something to help Maina and millions of children like her. But how does one person stop or even put a dent in slavery?

Chapter 3—Going Down

In the elevator of life, most people like to ride up. I'm told that the penthouse—the residence at the top floor of a building—is the best. The terrace on the roof has the most expansive view and it is closest to the sun. On the ride to the sky, people crowd into the small space and chatter as they ascend.

Conversely, few people choose to take a trip to the deepest levels of a multifloor basement. They don't go unless there is a compelling reason or force. Even on the sunniest day, it's dark underground. When the button gets pushed for a subterranean destination, sometimes the descent can seem solitary, silent, and lonesome.

The day I met Maina, I entered an elevator—the small room of knowledge that slavery—even worse, child slavery—still exists. Years later when Mark told me, ever so carefully, that eleven-year-old Maina had been forced into the sex trade when she was enslaved in the circus, my heart sank. I knew that Maina was one of the lucky ones—she was one of the few little girls who had been rescued. She now ate all the food she wanted and slept in a safe, warm bed. Her waking nightmare had ended. But I questioned whether she was truly lucky overall. When she was rescued, the special center for girls liberated from sex slavery was not yet in existence. Medical and psychological professionals were still seeking the best treatments for these fragile patients. Realizing Maina's memories or horrific dreams might never end, I sensed that the floors above ground were far away, yet I was still descending.

Chapter 4—The Unknown Horizon

At first after meeting Mark and Maina, when I returned to the United States, my life didn't seem noticeably different. Occasionally, Indian bracelets I had picked up at a bazaar jangled on my wrists as I worked at my computer. Every now and then an observation of India crept into one of my articles. People closest to me detected only a hint of the restlessness that comes from not knowing how old and new experiences fit together. For the most part, my routines appeared unchanged. Even the printed photo of Maina, tucked into my desk drawer, remained unseen by everyone but me ... for a while.

But any traveler will tell you, if you step just one foot off a trail and veer in a direction differing by just a few degrees, the scenery looks the same for only a few miles. Eventually you will discover that your familiar horizon is nowhere to be seen.

*

How does anyone fight slavery without a clue about how it starts, how it is perpetuated, and how it can be solved? Even before beginning a quest for information and answers, I had to grapple with all the emotions that accompanied my newfound realizations. I felt horror: What if Huro or Shivji had made my living room's pretty Oriental carpet I had purchased—with pride and thrill—for a price almost too good to be true? I felt naïve and sheepish: Did I think the term *human trafficking* was an invention for Hollywood movies? I also struggled with the remnants of a dream and memories of an earlier trip to India.

A month before I met Mark and Maina, I dreamed I met Mahatma Gandhi. Somewhere in a poor, southern US neighborhood we were playing basketball at a hoop at the end of a driveway. Neither of us could send the ball through the net, so we ended our game to sit and talk. We perched on wooden crates under an abandoned concrete carport. For a few minutes, we sat silently in the carport's shade, dark in contrast to the dazzling brilliant sunshine beyond the shadow of the roof.

Then Gandhi leaned toward me and looked me straight in the eye. "Thank you for taking care of my people," he said.

I woke feeling startled and astonished before I could ask a single question. Who were his people who needed help? How exactly was I supposed to take care of them? What was the message my unconscious mind was trying to convey to me through this vivid dream? Long after I had woken from the dream and months after I returned from my trip to the Taj Mahal and the center for children, the dream with its undecipherable puzzle replayed in my mind. It stubbornly refused to leave my conscious thoughts.

I also had to make sense of memories. My observations and experiences had not changed, but their meaning and implications had become topsy-turvy and needed to be reoriented. The memory of an unusual afternoon on an earlier trip stood out from other recollections, begging to be reexamined for insight.

A year before meeting Mark and Maina, my first trip to India and to a developing nation left me with a colorful photograph album and corresponding mental pictures. Sights I had perceived as simply quaint or fascinating activities at that time, however, became images that spurred strange questions after I had learned of the existence of modern slavery. There was more to those sights than what appeared on the surface.

In 2003, I'd ridden in the backseat of a car in southern India, heading off for a relaxing weekend of sightseeing after attending a workshop. The scenery rolled in front of me like a documentary film. A field of tattered gray tarps stretched on and on, not a foot of bare ground between each flimsy plastic roof. A low wall separated the bleak field from a hardened dirt shoulder strewn with worthless scraps of trash. An Indian driver whisked me down the road so quickly that the image became as gray and blurry as my dim recollections of a textbook where I had first encountered a *tent city*. As a student, a tent city had meant little more than a vocabulary term or a historical relic. Seeing one firsthand was hardly more elucidating. *Was that really a tent city?* With the unprepared mind of a protected life, how could I comprehend what I saw, much less give it a name that existed previously for me only as two words on a page?

We continued on the same stretch of pavement through a small village where the road's surface became jagged. We stopped once, just for a minute, while workers patched a pothole. I rolled down my window, trading a barrier from the sweltering heat, choking dust, and acrid smoke for a clearer view. From my spot in the backseat I watched women along the roadside smash rocks with heavy hammers to make gravel. Men tended a fire under a large cauldron. After a few men filled a gash in the road with various sizes of gravel, two others hoisted the pot from the fire and poured its steaming black contents over the stones and rough edges outlining the hole. When the men and their pot were back safely on the side of the road, we moved forward.

The driver and I continued into the countryside. I craned my neck to see the landscape through the windshield: red soil, emerald-green mulberry leaves, a cloudless blue sky, a tiny pink and blue house, and a man and several sacks of grain in a wooden cart pulled by a pair of yoked bullocks—huge bony beasts of burden with odd faces and horns. A tiny absurdity caught my eye. My curiosity ended the silence of our ride.

"Why did those bullocks have blue and orange horns?" I asked the driver.

He glanced at me. "What do you mean? Bullocks do not have horns," he replied politely, patiently, masking a hint of skepticism or, perhaps, confusion. He casually tooted the car horn along the now-deserted road. "A horn," he asserted. He looked over his shoulder at me to make sure I understood.

"Yes … ahhh, a horn. Well, what do you call these?" I asked, leaning nearly into the front seat and poking my index fingers over the top of my head to convey the appearance of an animal's horns.

"You mean their *sticks*, madam. Those are the bullocks' *sticks*," the driver emphasized with a smile. He seemed pleased to share his knowledge with me.

"But why are they blue and orange?" I pressed him.

A combination of amusement and kindness spread across his face. "Madam," he answered. "They do not grow that way. The farmer painted them for our January harvest festival. The paint has not yet come off."

I nodded and grinned. The painted sticks were a faint reminder of a celebration, like a leftover strand of Christmas tinsel dangling from a Vermont evergreen bough long past New Year's Day.

It had never occurred to me that the driver could think that, as a foreigner, I might believe that an animal could possess a horn or sprout blue and orange body parts. As I thought about how little any of us know about each other, I began to chuckle. Within moments, we were laughing together.

"Would madam prefer to sit in the front to see?" he offered. At my instant yes he stopped the car at the edge of the road and I climbed into the seat beside him.

We exchanged names—Gobi and Carol. For the next three hours, we swapped stories of our daily lives—our work and families in India and the United States. Gobi was extraordinarily proud of his son who was getting the secondary education that he had never received. I adored my husband and two daughters who were back home working and going to school. Gobi wanted to know about American politics and salaries. I wanted to know about native plants and the ladies in long, flowing blue saris who walked along the road, which had become a dirt lane.

Just before our trip ended, Gobi turned to me with a serious look on his face. "Madam Carol, there is something I have always wanted to know but have never been able to ask a Western person."

He hesitated. I held my breath.

"Hold out your hand," he instructed. Apprehensively, I did so. He took one hand off the steering wheel and held it near mine.

"See our hands?" Gobi said. "Yours is white and mine is brown. I have seen other people like you and I wondered: Why is your skin so pale? Is it because of the food you eat? Or is it because of the temperature of your country?"

It was my turn to ponder what he knew or didn't, what sort of foundation of knowledge he might have, and how, therefore, I might answer. "I am pale because my parents are pale," I explained. "No matter what I eat, I will remain this color. If I spend many hours in the sun, my skin will burn and turn red for a few days. If I spend many days in the sun, my hands will become darker, but they will never become brown like yours."

He seemed to be considering the information as we reached our destination.

Now, years later, I was again contemplating our conversation. What do humans really know about each other? Can the powerful, wealthy, educated population really understand the world of the downtrodden, poor, and illiterate? And vice versa? What do we really know about someone else's home, occupation, salary, schooling, traditions, beliefs—life in another's skin? Somewhere in that afternoon car ride—a glimpse of a tent city, a view of villagers repairing a pothole by hand, and a meeting with a taxi driver who had completed just five years of school—there were some answers about why some people became slaves and others didn't. I just didn't know what they were.

The strange mental images of my dream and memories nudged me to move forward—to leave the past, to become more engaged in the present, and to figure out a way into the future. So what else could I do but explore further?

Part II:

Seeking Solutions,
Learning to Lead

Chapter 5—Slavery 101, 2006

My next foray into the dark side of humanity took me just eight miles down the road. Kevin Bales, the world's top authority on modern-day slavery was giving a seminar at my daughters' school. I bought his most recent book at a shop in town and cemented myself in a chair in the school's auditorium.

Kevin Bales looked like the quintessential professor—short hair, tweed jacket, and tie. But he spoke with the knowledge, passion, urgency, and compelling story of a leader on a mission. Bales was one of the cofounders of Free the Slaves, a nonprofit organization with the mission to end slavery. A fellow Quaker, I learned, he and other cofounders had made a decision around a kitchen table to finish the job started by abolitionists centuries ago. Within moments he had hooked a teenaged academic audience, plus teachers and parents, with emotional candor and shocking truths that left us outraged. Within a few more moments, he was offering a constructive outlet for our anger—solutions to rescue twenty-seven million slaves worldwide and to prevent further victims.

Slavery, Bales said, could be prevented by ensuring that people are not vulnerable. When families are uneducated or destitute—

such as those earning fewer than three US dollars per day in developing nations—they are at risk. Parents who don't know when the next meal is coming and have little hope of keeping their children alive are at high risk for deception, exploitation, and enslavement of their children.

On the contrary, people who are literate, educated, employed, well-versed in human rights, and face little threat of becoming orphaned by natural disaster or displaced by war are at low risk for slavery. In short, they have options.

I left the lecture with a few more pieces of the puzzle and a list of reading material. Furthermore, I now knew of an organization that was making strides in slavery prevention and survivor rehabilitation. I could point to one successful group that was aiding grassroots organizations that conducted rescues, fought for legal justice and remuneration, helped survivors with recovery and rehabilitation, and protected children through education and the prevention of human trafficking.

I had learned how Huro, Shivji, and Maina had ended up in captivity and understood that Gobi's minimal education and employment as a cab driver defended his family against slavery. But I hadn't figured out any way to take action. Short of simply donating money, I was no closer to lending much of a hand.

Mark Little, on the other hand, had discovered some very practical avenues for helping and seemed eager to share what he had learned. Over the many months since our trip to the children's center, Mark and I had exchanged a few e-mail messages. Here and there he sent me a package—a videotape of a BBC television program about Huro and Shivji, and articles about slavery. He sent word about projects he and others accomplished for the ashram—blankets for the dormitories and new toilets for the campus. Before a friend and I had finished raising funds to contribute to a library at the center, Mark had spearheaded efforts that funded, constructed, and furnished it.

We discovered we had mutual friends through Rotary, an international organization of humanitarian volunteers. Rotarians and fellow travelers from our trip in 2004 to the Indian ashram bumped into each of us and passed along greetings.

In summer of 2008, Mark called from England with surprising news: he and his wife, Liz, were headed to the United States. They could visit after a weekend in New York City.

An idea simmered in the back of my mind as I prepared for their visit. Mark Little and Kevin Bales were committed to ending slavery and helping its survivors, yet much of the time the Atlantic Ocean separated them. What if I figured out a way for them to meet? I gathered up courage and e-mailed a message to Bales, brazenly inviting us to his office and for lunch during the short time that the Littles were staying at our home. Gracefully, he accepted.

On a sunny autumn day, the Littles and Metzkers piled into the car for a road trip to Washington, DC. The hours passed quickly with great conversation and much laughter. The visit with Bales, our time at Free the Slaves, and lunch that ended with profiteroles at a nearby little French restaurant flew even more quickly.

We talked around a small conference table at Free the Slaves' US East Coast center. We discussed the nonprofit organization's activities and Rotary projects Mark had coordinated in India. I observed and learned. Before we left, Mark asked Bales and a colleague, Ginny Baumann, a simple question: "What do you need?"

"Transportation for a boys' center in India," Ginny replied.

"That shouldn't be difficult," Mark asserted.

Most people know: if you fan two separate but nearby flames, anything in the middle of the two is going to ignite. I felt privileged to have introduced two people who could move mountains. What I didn't realize was that I had just been inducted into the circle of antislavery activists. My mental ember, sparked by meeting Maina and glowing faintly for a few years, had just become a fire.

Chapter 6—The Vintage Dress

Mark's words rang a bit crazy to me. Did he really say that providing a means of transportation for a shelter in India wouldn't be hard? No expert in raising funds, I had no clue how to find thousands of dollars to pay for a vehicle. And it couldn't be just any vehicle—the center needed something large enough to carry several children simultaneously. The vehicle had to be sturdy and reliable to navigate unpaved roads with crater-sized potholes in monsoon rains as reliably as it maneuvered smooth highway. We were also dealing with a need on the other side of the globe, in a country where bargaining for goods is an art and dealing in English isn't always a guarantee.

Yet Mark's cheery messages continued regularly. In England—five hours ahead of the US East Coast and my home—Mark would return home late at night after meeting with a Rotary club or church group, after some sort of creative fundraiser. He would e-mail or call me just after my suppertime with the news that he had received another donation of the equivalent of a few hundred dollars, sometimes more.

I wracked my brain for a way to raise money on this side of the Atlantic. We needed a compelling event and a type of fundraiser that hadn't already been done a hundred times in the community. The American economy had turned south in the fall of 2008 and people guarded their pocketbooks more closely than in the past. I also needed to find a segment of the population whose wallets hadn't been tapped repeatedly by a multitude of charities, all worthwhile and with an established local presence. To boot, I had no budget to stage a grandiose gala event, so every resource would have to be donated or exchanged for future favors.

The solution presented itself one dreary winter weekend while cleaning out a closet, contemplating upcoming expenses, and wishing for spring. With daughters finishing high school, balancing finances for college education with end-of-high-school expenses—graduation attire, college board fees, class activities, and prom dresses—was at the forefront of my mind.

Toward the back of the guest room closet my decades-old junior prom dress was still on a hanger. In back of it hung my aunt's formal gown from the 1950s. I snickered to think that the dresses—now with a few age spots and stiffening taffeta—were not just old and used but "vintage." I considered throwing them out but hesitated, partially because of their sentimental value and partially because I hated for them to take up space in a landfill.

Too bad the dresses couldn't be revived and worn again by someone, I thought. The price of a formal dress was about the same as a college textbook. In a recession, an expensive gown to wear just once was a luxury some girls could not afford.

In those thoughts lay the answer. I called Kathryn, my sixteen-year-old daughter, and asked if she thought the idea would fly.

Within weeks, she and I had secured space for an event at her school, and my Rotary club had agreed to run it. I had enlisted the help of nearly all the females I knew within a fifty-mile radius. I asked them to scour their attics and closets for gently worn, no-longer-used party dresses, wedding frocks, and jewelry. We would sell the donated party clothing to girls at rock-bottom prices; all proceeds would fund projects for survivors of human trafficking and slavery.

On March 28, 2009, the event Dress for a Good Cause was born. At last, I could e-mail Mark and Free the Slaves with news that my Rotary club could contribute toward the purchase of a vehicle for the boys' center and for a more immediate need that had just arisen—a motorcycle. Although a larger vehicle was still needed for raid-and-rescue operations, rides to court and medical appointments, and the return to home villages, a motorcycle would fulfill a different need. Field workers could visit children reunited with their parents to ensure that the families were still free, healthy, and thriving. On a motorcycle, long-distance trips would be economical yet speedy.

As word of the Dress event's fun and success spread, donations of clothing and accessories began to pour in from far and wide. Sequined, spangled, and beaded dresses arrived from consignment shops, women's centers, the costume department of People's Light & Theatre, dance classes, and churches. Nearby high school students and women who, for sentimental reasons, had once been unable to bear giving up their special dresses yet couldn't wear or store them any longer called to donate them. Contributions of pink prom dresses from each decade since the 1950s, a new woman's tuxedo imported from Italy, designer-label gowns, a Korean wedding outfit, and a treasure trove of jewelry overflowed my home and invaded the living rooms of women from my Rotary club.

A second Dress for a Good Cause event followed. Again we transformed a schoolroom into a dress shop with a party atmosphere. Soon the fundraiser launched at an additional location. Volunteers appeared and contributed, seemingly exactly what we needed at any given turn.

We began to learn just how powerful money could be and the benefits that even small amounts of funds could have for survivors of human trafficking and slavery. With the help of Free the Slaves, dollars from our Rotary club and British pounds from Mark Little's club in England were transferred to India and exchanged for rupees to purchase the motorcycle. Larger sums of money were earmarked for the vehicle.

Mark and I put our heads together for the next project. With the confidence of one successful project completed and another underway, I telephoned Ginny at Free the Slaves and asked what the survivors needed next.

Chapter 7—Traveling Companions

Convincing people to "ride the elevator" in the "wrong" direction with me was tricky business. Too much sad or scary information delivered too quickly overwhelmed listeners, sending them into a state of denial. Too little information communicated over too long a period led listeners to forget what they had heard. Too few options offered for helping them make change dulled their ability to hear, to feel moved, or to believe they could make a difference.

The hardest situation for me to accept was apathy. A few people, who spoke with certainty, told me some of my efforts were hardly worth the bother because slavery couldn't be eradicated until poverty was eliminated ... and that wouldn't happen in any foreseeable future. To me, their indifference, beneath the mask of a realistic attitude, felt as scary, contagious, and deadly as a plague. All I could hope for was a quick quarantine before it spread to me and to caring individuals who believed in possibilities for something different. If we all gave up and went home, what would happen to millions of people?

In some cases, friends simply couldn't bear the hurt of hearing about atrocities against other humans. Sometimes they had already experienced too much darkness in their own past; their own hidden horrors could not be unearthed without significant pain.

Yet I discovered open minds and sympathetic ears in unexpected places. In one case, a truck driver who traveled regular routes along mid-Atlantic highways said that her haul included a dashboard magnet with a hotline number to report suspected victims of child sex slavery at truck stops, notorious for illegal nighttime activities. In another case, I met a committee of businesspeople committed to bringing fair trade products—items made without slave labor in their supply chains—to their town.

Sometimes by accident, sometimes deliberately, travelers headed downward with me. Friends, family, Rotarians, teachers, dancers, artists, people strong in their faith, and other concerned folks took the elevator with me as often as they could. When insecurity over my "ordinariness"—my lack of fame, special status, or political power—reared its ugly head, allies' small yet significant signs of support pushed back my doubts. When the feeling that I was an outsider looking in at the people—paid educators, rescuers, or medical professionals—who did the "real" work and helped survivors heal threatened to become my excuse for my stopping at the next floor to take the stairs up, friends' help and companionship kept me going.

One day I grasped that my trip down wasn't as lonely as it sometimes felt. Compassionate, brave souls—Mark, workers at the ashram, Kevin, Ginny, and staff members at Free the Slaves, journalists, centuries' worth of abolitionists, and untold numbers of people whose names I didn't know—had ridden the elevator for a long, long time. They had traveled below ground long before

I had inadvertently pushed the button that sent the elevator to Maina's ashram.

On the most recent telephone call with Free the Slaves, I answered yes to their latest request for Rotarians' help. With that response, the elevator landed and doors opened to a floor where I had never been.

What Free the Slaves needed next was support for a new center for girls. Punarnawa Ashram, a special rehabilitation center in India, was being built for girls who were rescued from sex slavery. *Punarnawa*, translated as New Beginnings, would provide a safe haven, highly specialized medical and psychological treatment, education, vocational training, and compassionate care for minors who had been victims of adults' cold-blooded monetary and sexual desires. In an area where electricity was spotty, education for girls was outside the norm, and poverty was rampant, a host of challenges could be solved by an unlikely gift: a small herd of cattle and a "bio-gas" cooking system.

Thanks to Google, my Rotary club and I found mountains of information about cow manure and its transformation to become clean bio-gas to power a stove. Thanks to fresh donations of prom gowns and Dress for a Good Cause, plus a small matching grant from the Guy Gundaker Foundation, we collected funds to pay for construction of an underground *digester,* where methane gas was separated from dung to create fuel for cooking and compost for fertilizing crops. Through the generosity of many Quakers—religious descendants of some of the Underground Railroad workers who helped escaped slaves in the 1800s—we gathered enough money to purchase cows and a cowshed and to pay for vet bills and feed to get a small herd on its feet.

As funds and moral support for projects rolled in, so did supporters' and donors' questions. Was the motorcycle doing its job? Had we negotiated a good price for a vehicle for the rescued-boys' center? How many calves had been born at the shed at the girls' ashram so far? Photos and reports e-mailed from Free the Slaves' workers in India allowed us to celebrate the day that a coordinator took an inaugural trip on the motorcycle. Rotarians applauded the day the news arrived that the girls and caregivers cooked their first meal on the methane stove.

It wasn't long, however, before I realized the need to check on projects so I could answer donors' inquiries with firsthand knowledge. Intelligent and curious contributors wanted opinions and insight formulated from observations and reflection. It was time for another trip to India.

It became apparent that if I were to visit the boys' and girls' ashrams and potentially interact with survivors, I needed to learn more about communication—how to relate with the utmost sensitivity to their needs. That education might also provide fresh perspectives on speaking to groups of potential donors and unintentionally awakening memories of audience members who had experienced trauma or violence.

Looking for a mentor to help with that type of communication led to an unforeseen twist of fate.

Chapter 8—Surviving Crime

At a meeting one afternoon early in summer 2010, a guest speaker gave a presentation about the county's Crime Victims' Center. She talked about the grassroots organization that began in the 1970s with one phone, one desk, and a corps of volunteers dedicated to helping women who were victims of sexual assault and rape. During that era, reporting a rape was nearly unheard of and the notion of a victim advocate—someone to support a victim through procedures at the hospital, police station, or courthouse—was still on the horizon. With each step in advocacy, counseling, fundraising, and community building, the center broke new ground.

Over the decades, times changed and the center grew. Public sentiment transformed to recognize sexual assault as a crime of power against females and males of all ages. Blame shifted to the perpetrator instead of the victim. Committed staff, added when grant money became available, and volunteers forged relationships among the police force, social service agencies, the judicial system, and medical professionals. All the while they focused on helping victims obtain the medical, psychological, and legal help they needed to heal. The Crime Victims' Center expanded its services to ensure compassionate and skilled response to victims of all types of crimes, ranging from identity theft to rape and murder. It became a model agency for similar centers in Pennsylvania and Japan.

The invited speaker had barely moved from her spot in the limelight when I approached her. Would someone at the center teach me ways to talk with someone harmed by human trafficking, particularly sexual abuse and exploitation?

Within days, the center's training and volunteer coordinator called me. Would I come in for an interview to discuss attending their upcoming training sessions? A class for volunteer rape counselors and hotline responders, interns, and new advocates was beginning shortly.

The interview—a long conversation that delved into our personal beliefs, past experiences, my reasons for wanting to learn more about crime response, and my goals for communicating at the boys' and girls' centers in India—went well. It didn't end quite as I had anticipated it would, however. It concluded with an invitation to join their upcoming training program and a question: After the training, would I volunteer for the center's hotline?

At the end of the summer, I emerged with a title of junior rape counselor, a clearance, and a schedule of nights when I would be on call for the center. I also held a list of compassionate and intelligent senior counselors and staff, mostly young women who were wise beyond their years, who would continue to educate me as I gained experience over the next year.

The volunteer coordinator, experienced advocates, and therapists taught me alarming statistics about crimes, especially those of a sexual nature. A multitude of representatives from the district attorney's office, the county's department of child and youth services, domestic violence center, an HIV/AIDS clinic, and the local chapter of Mothers Against Drunk Driving provided knowledge and practical tips. They shared methods of coping with stress after listening to heartrending stories. A colleague at a publishing company mailed me a book about trauma stewardship in hopes that it would help me deal with my own emotions after helping with a victim's.

Although there was no specific training for helping survivors of human trafficking, the center's staff members coached me on ways to help people who might have similar situations—hotline callers who experienced flashbacks of crimes inflicted against their bodies or tearful victims who needed an ear or a shoulder to lean on for a few minutes. They taught me one of the most important statements for a survivor to hear and to internalize: "This was not your fault."

Experienced associates prepared me to visit a hospital emergency room with a victim: always accept a nurse's offer for coffee because a night with a victim of a sex crime would be long. Pack a bag with large T-shirt and sweatpants for a victim to wear home because clothing would need to be taken away and placed in an evidence bag. When a victim says the medical examination is too much to withstand psychologically, it is time to take a break or stop altogether.

Thankfully, emergency calls to the hotline when I staffed it were relatively few and far between. As much as I wanted to provide useful service during my allocated time, mornings after quiet nights I often breathed a prayer of gratitude that no one had experienced a terrifying, life-altering event that required the center's intervention.

But my occasional face-to-face visits with victims were sobering. What couldn't be completely taught through advice or books was the ability to remain strong when advocating for a sixteen-year-old rape victim whose date or evening of innocent fun had gone drastically wrong. There was no way to describe the feeling of sitting with a mother who would have given her life to protect her child against the sexual assault that had just occurred and to know that the comfort any counselor or I could give might help but would never be enough to take away all the hurt. Only experience could teach me ways to communicate volumes of support with my eyes to a distraught girl at a police interview during which only she and the detective were supposed to be heard on tape. I learned when to speak and when to listen—which was most of the time—to victims and survivors.

I developed huge respect and admiration for male officers who put away their weapons in an interview room, traded a no-nonsense demeanor for a gentle presence, and tried to learn as much about a crime as possible while attempting not to retraumatize or cause further harm to a frightened girl whose life had been turned upside-down. Real-life experience in a police station taught me just how deeply the heartache over a victim could be felt by families, officers, crime victim advocates, and all manner of community members. Even still, none of the pain a support team suffered could compare to the devastation endured by a victim.

Volunteers and staff at the Crime Victims' Center walked each day in this dark underground world. They supported people affected by crime, other workers who assisted victims, each other, and me. Surprisingly, they often managed to find humor over life's quirks and to remain lighthearted a great deal of the time.

The Crime Victims' Center's volunteer coordinator, along with friends, took my newfound enthusiasm for cow manure and methane in stride. Volunteers and staff also began to collect dresses for Dress for a Good Cause fundraisers. They encouraged me as I prepared for my trip to India, set for fall.

Plans took shape to see the motorcycle, hand over keys to the vehicle for the boys' center, and visit the newly built girls' center, where the first cows had moved into the new cowshed and a biogas system was under construction.

Messages and calls increased between the United States and England. Mark Little, now a constant companion in the cause, had kept in touch by e-mail weekly or monthly since our road trip to Free the Slaves. His charming and sometimes bawdy British humor often lightened our tasks and distracted me from uncertainties.

During what seemed to be an interminable wait for international colleagues to decide whether or not to help us negotiate the price of the vehicle, Mark sent a link to a video—documentary footage of a wild monkey grooming another, with the voiceover of a dentist alternately asking questions and reprimanding a patient for talking. Shortly after sending me a draft response to bureaucrats who seemed concerned that our speaking out against child slavery could spark unwanted international controversy, he forwarded a link to a satirical clip of flight attendants singing opera. One afternoon when I was wondering whether my volunteer efforts would amount to anything other than a diminished bank account, out of the blue he sent inspiring photographs with a message of reassurance. Once, he simply reminded me of a quotation often attributed to Mahatma Gandhi that I had once sent to him:

First they ignore you.
Then they laugh at you.
Then they fight you.
Then you win.

Now our correspondence was almost daily. To my great delight, Mark decided to join the trip. He recruited Stephen, another dynamic humanitarian and Rotarian from England, to come along. Ultimately, a dozen travelers from the United States, England, and Denmark arranged to gather in India. Reminiscent of my trip six years earlier, Rotarians and friends planned to tour ancient sites, drink in the colorful Indian pageantry in major cities and along the Ganges River, and confer about humanitarian projects across the globe.

My excitement overflowed. My suitcase was packed. My mind was prepared to learn more about the problems and solutions of human trafficking and to meet young survivors. A sturdy multipassenger vehicle for the boys' center, Bal Vikas Ashram, had been paid for with funds from the Rotary clubs in several countries and a matching grant from The Rotary Foundation. At the airport in Newark, New Jersey, I could almost will myself to feel the sweltering heat of sun-drenched afternoons and smell kerosene lamps, spicy rice dishes, diesel exhaust, and jasmine flowers before arriving in Delhi, India. Visits to the boys' and girls' rehabilitation and education centers were just a flight away.

Chapter 9—Liberated

"At my first raid-and-rescue mission, I was afraid," Rajneesh admitted. There was much at stake; there was no room for error. "If I failed, what would the consequences be for the children?"

His first rescue, conducted successfully in 2004 in the carpet industry in India, took a mountain of red tape and delicate preparation with authorities for an operation that lasted slightly fewer than fifteen minutes. It resulted in the release of fourteen children. "The children were smiling, saying they were happy to be released. Then I was happy," he recounted.

Six years later, the more confident yet genuinely humble man had participated in four hundred fifty rescues resulting in the rescue of more than two thousand slaves—"children, women, old people, girls … and I still feel the same happiness," the liberator said simply.

Crammed into seats without leg room at the back of yet another bus, Rajneesh and I talked about his work. Our team—tourists and concerned individuals—were on the way to Bal Vikas Ashram, a center at a remote location in India for boys rescued from slavery.

Rajneesh described the process of freeing slaves and some of the accompanying perils. Informants—alert, caring members of a community who notice something suspicious, or community activists from vigilance committees formed in villages where trafficking is prevalent—notify special coordinators about potential victims spotted in hidden places. Coordinators and field workers begin preparation, which can take two days to two months, to conduct a raid. Enlisting the required help from government authorities must be undertaken with the utmost care because if an official isn't sensitive to slavery—or worse, is corrupt—word of the raid will leak in advance, and the youngsters will be moved to another location in captivity. And who knows when the children might be found again by a sympathetic person with the knowledge and courage to sound an alarm?

Once appropriate legal paperwork is in place, representatives from labor and police departments, administrators from the Indian government, and field coordinators—such as Rajneesh—form a rescue team. They travel to the site of the rescue operation, where a raid takes place in twenty minutes or fewer. At any stage of preparation or during the raid, one brutal slaveholder, one official bribed to look in another direction or reveal sensitive information, or one violent thug can cause slaves to be taken away or further abused, or rescue team members to be discovered and beaten. A raid that doesn't go well can have severe repercussions.

Bus-ride conversations were interrupted as we passed a tractor hitched to a house-sized burlap bag of processed grain with seven men standing on top; we stopped to gawk and take pictures. Moments later we stretched our legs at a village where female team members greeted young mothers with cute babies and we all watched workers carry bundles of millet.

Rajneesh and I resumed chatting as our bus trip continued over bridges and past the tiniest of temples, camel carts, and fields. Not one child at the ashram had been sold into slavery by a family member, he told me. Poor families who cannot afford enough food for their children are easily deceived by traffickers who promise education, food, and a home for a boy in return for a couple hours of work each day. The boys at the center had been rescued by Rajneesh or other liberators, or had escaped. After family visits and with the consent of the parents, they go to the ashram for treatment, rehabilitation, and education.

After a long trip, we rolled down a long, secluded lane and into a gated courtyard. Thirty-three boys ages ten to fifteen, rescued from stone quarries, hotels, the garbage industry, and carpet, plastic, and brick factories welcomed us. These boys weren't sad and subdued, however. They were excited—smiling, waving, and running in all directions. Adults gathered the children to the side of the yard as we drew close and parked. The team climbed off the bus, some members taken by the hand by a child as we were all led into a building.

Plastic chairs awaited us at the front of a multipurpose room. Our backs against a blackboard and a poster of a foreign-language alphabet, we faced the boys and their caregivers and looked toward rows of neat bunk beds covered in woven spreads at the back of the long room.

Introductions aside, the speeches were few. The songs were many. Although English is one of the national languages of India, Hindi and other native tongues were spoken in the room; music conveyed messages of hope and love far more easily and effectively than translated monologues. The boys sang for our group, shyly at first, and then with full hearts and great gusto.

During one song, they raised their index fingers high into the air. "We are number one!" they belted out. It was no insignificant gesture for young men who had previously been stripped of their rights, dignity, self-esteem, and freedom.

Out of the corner of my eye, I noticed tears trickling down Mark's cheeks; a few of my own spilled down my face. The emotions of elation for the boys' current security, devastation over knowledge that they had previously experienced violence and captivity, humility in the presence of enormous compassion and strength, and joy that we could spend a few hours together were too immense to remain in my head.

Team members produced small gifts for the boys—balloons, colorful new cotton button-down shirts, and bright rubbery wristbands shaped like animals, plus a cheerful patchwork quilt presented to a small boy rescued just days earlier. With little fanfare—a later ceremony was set for the official bestowal—we handed over keys to a shiny, new-smelling SUV with sturdy tires and a first-aid kit for the backseat. The boys beamed at their new shirts and clamored to see each other's wristbands. Any serious, bashful, or formal tones of the morning evaporated and the musicians grabbed drums and keyboard again.

Unprompted, the boys formed a circle with a large center. One by one, they leapt into the ring and danced to joyous music. Within moments Mark, Stephen, and Arne from Denmark joined them in a spontaneous celebratory dance—of happiness, freedom, and life. The activity continued merrily, lasting until the call to lunch.

Chapter 10—Food for Thought

By the time I had strolled to the kitchen, filled a plate, and then made my way to sit cross-legged on the cool floor of a concrete porch, the boys were already engrossed in the meal. With great intensity and happiness, they dug into mountains of food covering large plates. Small thin boys put away great mounds of rice and pools of lentil soup. Taller teens quickly plowed through colorful side dishes of substances completely unfamiliar to me Then they looked up at me and grinned. I wondered where bodies so slim could put so much food.

Yet the meal was so quiet I could have heard a pin drop. The boys' joy of eating all the food they could want and hold was tangible and present everywhere on the porch. As Kevin Bales had explained during his 2006 lecture at my children's school, and I was now seeing firsthand, a lot of healing can occur when a child on the brink of starvation gets enough food to replenish his body and psyche.

When the boys had eaten portions five times the size of the generous helpings on my plate, they jumped up and washed their dishes at large plastic tubs on the opposite side of the courtyard.

A tower of fragrant orange sections appeared near their washing station, and the boys dug in. Only after the plates were shining, and nothing was left of the oranges but peels headed for composting did the cacophony of boys at play begin again.

Ashram staff and some of the older residents led team members on a tour of the campus. Several boys beamed as they showed us their sewing machines and demonstrated their new skills as tailors. Others proudly led the foreigners to see classrooms and workshops where they learned reading, writing, bicycle repair, and carpentry.

While team members continued their tour of the grounds, with the help of a translator and under the sensitive supervision of caregivers, I talked briefly and carefully with three of the boys. They told me their names. They told their stories simply.

Smiling shyly, gentle Amrit* took my hand with both of his and searched my eyes before he spoke. He was twelve years old and had been rescued from a brick factory.

Before quiet Ravi* was freed, for four months he arose before dawn and was working with melted plastic before 6:00 a.m. each day. He and other boys enslaved at a plastic factory worked together to cook their too-small rations of rice in too-short allotments of time. One group of boys started the fire and process of cooking rice while the others worked; the second group finished cooking the rice and served all of them after the boys in the first group had returned to their labors.

Young, spunky Mahabala ran away from captivity. Forced to clean rooms and serve customers at a hotel from sunrise until 1:00 a.m.—often arising from sleep in the hours between 1:00

and sunrise, if a patron demanded attention—he once refused to work. His slaveholder tied him to a tree and beat him. Shortly thereafter, Mahabala escaped and found his way to train tracks. Concerned police officers spotted him and placed the call that resulted in his safety at Bal Vikas Ashram. Shirt untucked and bare feet dusty from playing in the dirt, he grinned as he left our conversation to participate in games with the other boys. I noticed that his permanent teeth were still growing in.

When the boys shifted the conversation, looked away, or began to fidget, adults quietly, in English, filled in a few of the details for my notes. It was apparent that when the children got close to memories of violence, they needed to change the subject. No one pressed; the discussion moved to safer ground. Even a momentary shadow across a young survivor's face was deemed to last too long.

Their stories, although each unique in details, were representative of those of other boys at the center. Two were new to Bal Vikas Ashram and still slightly disoriented in early stages of freedom. Some were making a transition from dependence on caregivers to self-reliance. Others, in final stages of recovery, were ready to return with new shields of education, job skills, and knowledge of their human rights, to welcoming homes and villages. A couple of boys, whose migrant parents had not yet been located or who were orphaned, would remain at Bal Vikas as long as they needed a home.

The boys' stories and demeanor were a testament to the human spirit. Although they had endured horrendous ordeals and experienced terrible harm inflicted by ruthless slaveholders, they demonstrated a great will to survive. In a new place where caregivers loved them and helped them mend, the boys thrived. They were already moving forward.

Stuffed with much food for thought, I was ready to lighten my frame of mind and to play. Well-fed physically and emotionally, the rest of our international band was also eager for fun. Americans pulled bubble solution and wands from backpacks and taught the boys how to blow bubbles. Mike Korengel, a man from my town who was on his first trip to India, presented the final gift of soccer balls, resulting in great glee.

Soccer balls and echoes of toots of a horn bounced off the center's buildings. Mike and others played soccer with the boys. A Rotarian with an Indian driver's license drove up and down the ashram's driveway with young passengers excited to ride in the new vehicle. As kids waved out the windows of the SUV, our gift seemed for a few minutes more like the gift of a theme-park adventure ride than transportation for the serious missions it would undertake after our team left.

Reluctant to end our visit, we formed two long lines leading to the door of our bus: ashram residents in one queue and foreign guests in another. To say good-bye, team members shook hands and spoke to each member of the other line. One by one we gradually moved back to our vehicle. One by one the rejuvenated travelers, as effervescent as the bubbles blown by the boys moments earlier, seemed to float back onto the bus.

I had just experienced one of the most sublime days of my life. Being with boys whose human spirit was alive and well was uplifting. Delivering the vehicle—making a difference in the lives of these survivors and more to come—was a dream come true. Thanks to Mark Little, Rotarians in many countries, and everyone who had helped with Dress for a Good Cause, all our efforts had paid off. With the victory came the realization and the proof that change not only could occur, it *was* occurring. My hope and belief, that we could make a dent in slavery during my lifetime, solidified.

My euphoria peaked as one of the coordinators and I clasped hands to say farewell. We stood in solidarity—together with our friends—to improve the circumstances of twenty-seven million slaves, beginning with the children around us.

Chapter 11—The Fall

Unfortunately, the glow from the day did not last. While parts of the visit to India had been rocky, within hours of our departure from the ashram, the trip began to completely fall apart. The intense smog burned my nostrils. As with several of my traveling companions, my stomach began to rebel against food—perhaps from jet lag, perhaps impure water ingested accidentally, or food that was simply foreign to my digestive system. Exhaustion from long days of travel, walking on village lanes past open sewer ditches and freely roaming pigs that ate from garbage piles, and a late night caused by a broken-down bus caught up with me. An overnight journey in a cramped third-tier train bunk— adventurous and far off the beaten path of typical tourism, but hardly conducive to decent sleep—left me short on energy reserves and susceptible to sickness.

My last straw came during check-in to our small village hotel. The promised new facility was beyond anything imaginable by our group of Western tourists. We climbed flights of grimy stairs to reach our rooms. My bed was clothed in dirty sheets; other travelers' beds were bare mattresses. A teakettle crusty with filth sat on the chest of drawers. The toilet—a harbor for mosquitoes—seemed little more than a hole in the tile floor with a pipe that led to the ground several stories below. Electricity was intermittent; I didn't let go of my flashlight.

The team was already weary and beyond its comfort zone; many travelers had begun to complain of health problems even beyond digestive disorders. Most of us were miserable and at wits' end with the conditions of the accommodations. Some team members grumbled to me, with just cause. Others yelled and swore.

One of our most good-natured stalwart participants approached me in tears. "Carol, this is unacceptable," she said. I could do nothing but concur and apologize, for there was no other facility in the village for relocating. Overwhelmed with obstacles, frustrated at my inability to make any improvements, I berated myself for dragging myself and others into a mess. Sometime past midnight, after failing at attempts to deal with situations over which I had no control, I went to bed wearing my day's disheveled clothes and cried in the dark.

We continued on our way to slightly brighter facilities and sightseeing adventures along the Ganges River, but my body had had enough. Back in Delhi, I felt too sick to keep going and retreated from the street to the hotel. I caught a glimpse of myself in the elevator mirror; my face didn't look familiar. Midafternoon, feeling anxious, nauseous, and completely unlike myself, I crawled into bed and stayed. The crash came hard, physically and emotionally.

By evening I had bowed out of the rest of our activities. Indian friends called a doctor, but the word was that if my antibiotic didn't work, there wasn't much else to be done.

Chapter 12—Longing for Home

Lying in the dark, I tried to focus on something happy, something positive, something other than hurting. Anything other than hurting. It was impossible. My stomach was trying to turn inside out. My joints and skin prickled, maybe from fever.

Worse than the ache of my body was the ache in my heart. I was lonely. I missed my family. I wanted to bury my face in my husband's shoulder and listen to my daughters' voices. I missed my bed with clean, soft sheets. I missed my town with its pure water, fresh air, neighborhoods with tidy houses, and yards bordered by abundant fields and trees.

My town—where there were few crumbling walls, no rats scurrying in the corners of restaurant dining rooms, no sows and their piglets eating scraps of garbage piled in the streets. No linens washed in a river brimming with toxins. No half-clothed children with thick coughs. There I was again, focusing on the negative—my anxiety, my unhappiness, my nausea.

A twinge of my gut sent me to the toilet in the next room. Its flusher didn't work properly, but at least this hotel's toilet wasn't a tiled hole in the ground guarded by mosquitoes. What little rice, chai, and toast I had eaten over the last two or three days, for I had lost my appetite earlier, was gone.

All I could think about was going home. In the depths of my longing and misery, however, one stark truth kept me from pure self-pity. Not far away, there were children—tens of thousands of them—who were quickly losing any hope, any prayer, any dream of returning to their families and villages. They were never going home.

*

Without a pharmacy on every corner, as we were accustomed to in the United States, Mike Korengel scrounged up a glass of lemon juice and salt from the hotel kitchen to replace electrolytes. He arranged for my trip back to the States on the next day's flight.

Mark made preparations to continue to the girls' center without me. Supriya, who was to take Mark and me to the girls' ashram, sat on the side of my bed for our first face-to-face meeting. Before Mark and Supriya headed out for a flight east, I handed both of them some gifts to deliver to the ashram and mumbled my regrets for backing out. I was foggy and vague as we said good-bye.

I felt so bad that the wheelchair ride across the airport terminal was a blur. Normally a private person, I was so worn out that I didn't much care when people stared as I stretched out on the floor near the gate. After boarding the plane, I slept for the fifteen-hour flight back to the United States, not even waking for food.

Chapter 13—Ambivalence

The sight of my family's faces—my husband, Eric, and both daughters home from college for the Thanksgiving holiday—had never seemed so wonderful. Our family doctor, informed by Eric in advance that I might not be arriving in one piece—was on call if I needed help. Clean linens, warm pure water, and impeccable sanitation were a welcome relief.

Gratitude for everything I called home washed over me like a river. It felt like I could sleep for days on end, and for a few weeks I kept to an abbreviated work schedule.

Yet the months after my trip were a muddle of emotions. I was elated to have visited the boys' ashram in Allahabad. I felt jubilant to have participated in a ceremony to hand over keys to a vehicle for raid-and-rescue operations. At the same time, I felt overwhelmed by memories of sickness and conditions of poverty. I felt somehow partially responsible for my fellow travelers' illnesses; back in England, Mark had ended up in the hospital. Although I had experienced sights and signs of developing nations many times before, conditions on this trip had seemed worse. It was as though my traveling companions and I had stepped off tourism's marble staircase into a dirt pit of reality.

For six solid weeks I vowed I would never return to India. My resolve was trumped by regret. I was bitterly disappointed at missing the trek to the girls' ashram. As a female, as mother of two daughters, my heart was with the girls' center and my body hadn't reached it. I often questioned my lack of perseverance and strength—perhaps I only imagined I was too sick to go. I wondered whether I had been overdramatic about my health. Simultaneously, I could not face another trip, yet I yearned to try again to reach the girls' shelter.

A clean bill of health from my doctor received only seven weeks after my trip home and friends' reassurances assuaged some of my sadness and doubts. But every now and then, questions nagged at my conscience. *Wasn't there something I could have done to board the plane to the east where the center was located?*

Long after I felt physically well, emotional side effects lingered. Self-doubts, stronger than ever, were harder to shake. Relentlessly, I demanded justification for my desire to help: *Was I compensating for underlying guilt or feelings of unworthiness for leading a privileged life? Did I really know what I was doing or was I kidding myself? What did it even mean* to make a difference— *maybe,* I bitterly thought, *that was just a hollow string of words.* For a while it seemed easier to think negatively instead of positively about my role.

Callously, I dismissed the possibility that I had taken up previous Quakers' mantle of abolition because of strong empathy and ability to communicate. It didn't occur to me that my simultaneous strength and vulnerability—intense sensitivity to other peoples' feelings, such as the pain of survivors whose vulnerabilities led to their forced servitude—led me to serve them. I almost forgot that often optimism and idealism win.

The trip to India had consumed hours of planning and travel, dollars and energy. I could hardly just pull a few things together and go again. It wasn't as though I had missed a trip to New York and could hop aboard another train the next day. Feeling oddly stranded in my own country, I sought another avenue to help.

It was in that quest for personal connections, to learn more and to take action that I turned my sights on my own country and my own county. If slavery was worldwide and there were great pockets of wealth and poverty outside my front door, the issue of trafficking and slavery was probably right under my nose. Illegal, hidden, and rarely addressed by most people in my community, slavery and people fighting it nearby proved frustrating and difficult to find.

All of a sudden I felt like I was fighting insurmountable obstacles—a problem that was too big to tackle: survivors in the States too hard to find to help, survivors overseas too far away to reach, too much societal apathy and not enough money or energy to counter it, and a personal inability to figure out where I belonged in all the chaos. My disappointment rose like a flash flood and threatened to drown me.

On a gray Friday afternoon, a hair's breadth away from giving in to feelings of futility, and foolishly, by my own admission, I gave God an ultimatum. It was childish, self-centered, and specific: if, by the following Tuesday, I didn't receive some sort of sign that I should keep going with this quest, I was quitting.

On Monday, the phone rang. A coordinator at a local residence for survivors introduced herself. Through a string of telephone and e-mail messages, she heard I might lend a helping hand.

Part III:

Taking Action, Making Change

Chapter 14—Outside My Front Door

You don't just wake up one day, decide to take a batch of cookies to the local shelter for victims of slavery and human trafficking, pop a tray into the oven, and drive the warm baked goods to a location known by everyone in town. Unlike many charitable organizations that seek daily to be found, noticed, and aided, groups that help survivors walk a tightrope. They balance privacy, anonymity, and secrecy for security, with openness and publicity necessary to raise community awareness and funds for sustainability.

During my search for answers about slavery, a friend and fellow Rotarian had introduced me to a professor named Ron Chance. Chance was a former director of intelligence analysis for the US Department of Labor, where he investigated sweatshops and human trafficking in the workforce. He had helped form taskforces to rescue and restore victims of human trafficking in a couple of large cities along the US East Coast. I pulled his contact information from an old wrinkled business card and placed a call. The number still worked.

It was Chance who revealed to me the reality of slavery just miles from my front door. The hideous picture he painted—of organized crime, of Philadelphia as just one city on a national circuit for young girls bought and sold and forced into the sex trade, of despicable brutality against vulnerable people—was in sharp contrast to the beautiful, bucolic landscapes around my home. The dark, loathsome stories of deceit and violence were out of character with the bright, peaceful region I knew. Cases on the FBI's website and archived media articles corroborated the information he gave me.

He cited examples of slavery not far from my front yard. In June 2010 four brothers were arrested for smuggling young Ukrainian workers into Philadelphia. (They were convicted in October 2011.) The brothers forced them to work without pay— using violence and threats against their children—as nighttime cleaners in discount department stores. These crimes took place not in India, not in Haiti or Africa, but in Philadelphia, thirty miles from my door.

And he gave other examples: of thirty Russian women—victims of trafficking, homeless and desperate for help—who showed up at an agency in Wilmington, Delaware, that works toward prevention and treatment of AIDS. In another instance, a health worker reported that at his apartment building in southeast Pennsylvania, men lined up at a specific door every weekend. When authorities investigated the situation, they discovered that eight Mexican women were being held and forced to work in the sex trade.

In southeast Pennsylvania, outside Philadelphia, the most common industries for utilizing slaves are the sex trade, and agriculture and food processing, Chance told me. "Some [victims] are smuggled into the country, promised jobs as cooks or nannies," he said. "They come from Mexico and Latin America,

Asia, the former Soviet states, and Eastern Europe. They come for the promise of a better life in America, more money, equal rights, and education. They're desperate for a better situation, so they're vulnerable to deception."

All too quickly the promises dissolve and victims find themselves enslaved. With their passports taken away, unable to speak English, and without any support system, he explained, there is next-to-no hope of escaping and asking for help.

Chance highlighted changes, instigated by a local coalition, to help potential victims. He described local efforts to protect and help people rescued from slavery.

Our conversation changed my naïve view of my home, of human trafficking, and the unintended consequences of globalization. Slavery no longer existed solely in far-off places; it touched my neighborhood. My community wasn't too different from other cities around the United States where Lincoln's Emancipation Proclamation needed enforcement more than a hundred years after its inception. My discussion with Ron Chance also resulted in a string of phone calls for me to track down ways to help local survivors.

Many conversations and several weeks later, I had overcome hurdles to finding organizations that aided survivors of trafficking near my home. Armed with knowledge and a track record of providing help for survivors, and the assurance of support from Rotarians and friends, one day in early spring I found myself on a local train headed for a residence for female survivors. My backpack was stuffed with children's early readers—short picture books with one-word captions or simple, repetitive sentences—a small gift for women learning English.

The train rolled past suburbs with fancy shops, toward the city skyline, and then burrowed underground. It stopped at several busy stations where workers in suits and students in university sweatshirts checked their cell phones as trains pulled in and departed. Fewer travelers remained on board as we rose from deep tunnels to a landscape with a desolate train yard, crumbling buildings covered in graffiti, and postage-stamp gardens in a block strewn with litter. It continued farther until the terrain was unfamiliar and I wasn't quite sure of my bearings.

Greeted at the station by a cheerful program coordinator, I was whisked by car to a pretty, old home tucked into a block with row houses—some occupied, some vacant—in a neighborhood teeming with diversity. People out and about, walking to nearby shops or public transportation stops kept to their business and paid us little attention.

Entering the door of the home for survivors, I felt the calm of a sanctuary yet the hum of activity. A group of ladies, Asian I surmised, sitting around a kitchen table greeted me. They looked older and more careworn than I'd expected; I could not begin to guess their ages. Yet they seemed happy in the moment, chatting with each other in a language I didn't recognize. I peeked into a pot that the ladies checked on regularly; strange-looking potatoes or another unidentifiable vegetable boiled in bubbling water.

The two women who ran the residential program offered me a cup of tea, and we sat at the dining room table to talk. The home, they told me, had been established two years earlier. Founded to offer safety and rehabilitation for local and international women who had been victims of human trafficking, slavery, and commercial sexual exploitation, it had sheltered residents from Latin America, Indonesia, and the United States. Survivors arrived at the house through referrals from immigration services and the local police force. There, women received medical and psychological treatment, privacy, and peace to heal. When ready, they would learn job skills enabling them to lead self-sufficient lives with dignity and control over their decisions and actions.

Echoing Mark Little's simple question at Free the Slaves two years earlier, I asked, "What do you need?" The question now rolled easily off my tongue with the knowledge that somehow, whatever they requested would be possible given enough time.

They replied they needed money for heating bills, replacement wingback chairs for the ones with broken legs in their parlor, mattresses and other furniture, and funds to pay interpreters for languages rarely heard in my neighborhood. I remembered the small collection of easy-reading books stuffed in my backpack and quickly pulled them out to give to the directors. The survivors also needed companionship—the chance to practice English, learn American customs, and develop healthy relationships in an accepting atmosphere. Now slightly less of a novice at fundraising and better equipped to interact with victims of crime, I could comfortably assert, "That shouldn't be too difficult."

Before leaving the house to head back to the train station, I sat in the parlor to reorganize my backpack and thoughts. Two young blonde women joined me in the room and turned on the television. They asked where I was from, and then chatted a few moments before turning their attention to a rerun of *Law and Order* about a sex crime.

Trying to remain impassive, I stole a glance at the women's faces. They watched with the nonchalant expressions of slightly bored viewers waiting for a little excitement from a Hollywood soap opera—not a hint of distress or recognition. I stifled my own emotions of confusion and bewilderment. *How can they watch so dispassionately? Am I really watching a show about victims with victims?*

Voices interrupted my thoughts about the irony of the situation, watching a television version of women's lives with real victims, and the surreal nature of seeing the evidence of the hideous truth about slavery in my seemingly paradise-like area.

"I see two purple flowers." A chorus of voices slowly chanted the words of a book I had delivered. "I see two red flowers." Their accents told the story of coming from faraway places. The sound of survivors' voices faded as I retraced my steps back to the car and prepared to catch the return train home.

Chapter 15—Hanging by a Thread

For someone who thinks a thread is only something to hang by, I spent a lot of time with a needle and fabric in my hands. It took me ten minutes to stitch my great-aunt's clip-on earring—a fifty-year-old large blue trillium with a glass bead in the center—onto a small, colorful quilt. Despite my lack of skill with a needle, I had spent three hours walking a group of women through the steps of cutting and sewing pieces of the quilt face. Prior to that gathering I had spent hours of spare time salvaging scraps of fabric, picking the brain of my daughter who quilts, and hand-drawing rainbow-color-coded instructions for patchwork wall hangings. It was oddly satisfying work. Undoubtedly, the outcome—a tapestry of exquisite design and an explosion of color—was beautiful.

*

I took the coordinators' request for regular, ongoing opportunities for companionship seriously. Although university students' occasional activities with the ladies—often to gain experience in social work and for college credit or service-hour requirements—were enjoyable, the visits were too inconsistent or short-lived to allow genuine long-term relationships to develop. Furthermore, the survivors had experienced a darker side of life that left them with the perspectives of older souls. For them, companionship might come more easily with people whose laugh lines around the eyes were deeper and reactions to stress had been tested over a decade or two.

I chose a handful of remarkable female friends who were strong, accepting, mature, kind, trustworthy, and discreet and invited them to join me. I asked them to undergo background checks in order to visit a home with an undisclosed address. They agreed to help and to commit to recurring visits, no small feat in an age when opportunities to spend time are nearly infinite. Their faith in me—that I knew what I was doing—and their dedication to a cause and to women who needed their help was significant.

The small group of volunteers from a variety of Rotary clubs, churches, and professions promised to give time, attention, and effort over several months to form a friendship group. We sought an activity that would interest women of a range of ages and could be accomplished without a common language, skill, or talent. My older daughter Elizabeth came up with a solution: a plan for making a small, simple quilt. Then we set a date for survivors and volunteers to assemble around two sewing machines.

Our first gathering was held at the dining room table where I had first met the residence's coordinators. But the meetings could not have been more different. There was great commotion at the beginning of our quilting bee. Ten women crowded around sewing machines, scissors, pins, rulers, pencils, and spools of thread. Fabric scraps were everywhere—draped over chair backs, littering the floor, and scattered about the table.

Only one of the ten participants had ever quilted. Most had little sewing experience. So we spent several minutes figuring out who was able to tackle certain tasks and a few more minutes putting pieces together through trial and error. We ripped out more than a few seams and redid them.

The women hailed from five countries. We spoke even more languages; some were in the earliest stages of learning English. So we passed information and gestures around the table like we were playing the children's game of "whisper down the alley," hoping that the message sent was the same received.

Without a budget, salvaged scraps of fabric and trim from damaged or stained dresses left over from Dress for a Good Cause became the patchwork pieces we used. The chaos at the beginning of the sewing session—a hubbub of chattering women overeager to put scissors to use—settled into a happy engagement on simple tasks. Measure. Cut. Pin. Sew. Iron. Repeat. Piece by piece, the fragments took shape as a geometric pattern.

As we did with the cloth squares and triangles, bit by bit we figured out how we fit together as project participants and as friends. Nadira* was gifted with the ability to figure out which shape should connect with another and to sew straight, even seams. Narbelung's* lovely, gentle aura that exceeded her small frame provided a sense of tranquility as we worked. Young, bubbly Yana* easily leaned across the table to make suggestions to anyone who would follow her instructions and kept many of us laughing. Amicable Connie kept to the ironing board, happy to help out in a way that didn't involve the sewing machine. Ati* secretly hoarded tiny leftover scraps and handed them to Gina to fasten; we looked toward the end of the table partway through our quilting bee to discover Ati hugging a crooked strip of mismatched shapes and fabrics to her chest. She and Gina smiled sheepishly.

Three hours after we began, the group emerged with two completed quilt faces with stunning colors and remarkably pretty designs. We exclaimed over the geometric sunburst of green, peach, blue, red, and orange satin, and a bold red, silver, black, and white pinwheel.

When we departed, we took the completed quilt faces, ready to be attached to backing and stitched into completed tapestries. We left a large grocery bag of remaining fabric, a tool that looked like a pizza cutter, and a thin plastic cutting board.

We embraced in the manner of women who had known each other for three years, not three hours. The laughter, the warmth in the room that belied a cold front and thunderstorm that had blown in nearly unnoticed while we focused on our task, and the good-bye hugs signaled to me we had accomplished a simple goal. We had demonstrated we could have fun and enjoy each other's company while working together to create something pretty.

My daughter Elizabeth and another volunteer outside our group attached the quilt backs and finished the wall hangings. For fun, I stitched my great-aunt's earring at the center of the sunburst. The results were spectacular. Beyond two charming quilts, the group had formed the beginnings of a special friendship connected by threads of laughter, shared tasks, a common purpose, and fun.

Chapter 16—A Circle of Friends

Over the next several months, survivors and volunteers met regularly. We created a few more quilts and strung beaded bracelets. We put together a mobile of origami cranes— miniature birds created through the Japanese art of folding paper. Yana hung it at the house.

We visited nearby world-famous botanical gardens, thanks to the generosity of the venue's executive staff. Volunteers and survivors strolled along paths of sculpted shrubs and exquisite roses and through conservatory rooms bursting with orchids and hibiscus. Unable to photograph survivors' faces for the sake of their privacy and security, we took pictures of our feet around a quaint old sundial.

"America, America!" Nadira shouted. She shook her head in wonder at the beautiful blooms and fountains.

We made special note of Ati's improvement in English at the end of our tour. "When should we get together again?" the volunteers asked.

"Tomorrow," Ati replied comically. "We come here tomorrow."

With each visit, our friendship grew. We began to feel as comfortable sitting with each other in silence as we did when we chattered. On a walk during one visit, I saw Ati slip her hand into Connie's as though they had been girlfriends since childhood. We celebrated small victories, cried together over the death of family members, ate fresh dumplings regularly made by one of the survivors, and made a fuss over each other's triumphs and trials. A woman outside our group dubbed us the Circle of Friends, and the name stuck.

Over the months, Rotarians, Quakers, and friends continued to contribute pennies and dollars for projects, and we found ways to leverage and match funds brought in at Dress for a Good Cause. New reading lamps, comfortable chairs, and tables requested during my first visit became familiar furnishings in the home. Additional easy books landed on the coffee table, and an envelope with funds for a new washing machine arrived in the mailbox.

The publisher of a local magazine for women graciously printed articles announcing fundraisers and celebrating accomplished projects. One article was about the proprietor of a local quilt shop who invited the Circle of Friends to display one of its finished quilted wall hangings in an outdoor quilt show. Our little red, black, and silver pinwheel quilt blew in the breeze along with blanket-sized, fine hand-stitched award-winning spreads crafted by renowned quilters. Although our quilt took no prize at the exhibit, it was a triumph in our eyes.

Raising funds and holding activities for our Circle of Friends kept me busy. However, I still felt a compelling need to make it to the girls' rehabilitation center in India. I wanted to see the cows we had paid for; my curiosity about the workings of the bio-gas system was getting the better of me. There was a new project underway—the construction of a pavilion to allow gatherings and classes to be held outdoors, yet protected from monsoon rains and intense sunshine—and I was interested in its progress.

A small voice inside my head pushed me relentlessly to try the trip again. It implored me to understand firsthand the impact of efforts of the numerous men and women who conduct rescues, provide funds, and administer treatment to girls. It asked me to try once more to take a closer look at ways to aid girls who have undergone, perhaps, the worst kind of slavery of all—sex slavery. My soul needed to come face-to-face with the reality of survivors and parts of a puzzle to create a different future for, potentially, millions of people.

Finally, in the wake of my burning desire to visit the girls, my vow not to return to India completely dissolved. I sat down at my computer to check airline prices and new visa requirements.

Knowing from past experience that the right traveling companions can ease navigation through India, I recruited two adventurers with previous experience in India and flexibility when inevitable changes in plans occurred. They possessed cool-headed problem-solving skills and extreme good nature even when faced with hotel rodents, strange food, and transportation hiccups. The unflappable Mike Korengel, who had helped me onto the plane after the previous year's disastrous trip to India, signed up for the journey within seconds after I asked. Kathryn, my nineteen-year-old daughter, got the buy-in from professors to miss more than a week of classes at the University of Miami and brought a wealth of knowledge about the subjects of her major studies—international relations, environmental science, and anthropology.

A close family friend, who was born in India, invited us to visit his hometown and attend a wedding with him after our visit to the girls' center. He helped with arrangements and watched over the planning phase with the fastidious eye of a scientist and the care of a guardian angel.

I bought another ticket and threw gifts and my Indian clothing into my suitcase. After months of preparation, I was ready to go again.

My excitement escalated, but so did my misgivings. Rational and irrational fears raised ugly heads—*would I get sick again*? Afraid I might succumb to a dreadful disease, I told Eric that I wanted him to remarry if I died; absurdly, I listed women who were up to my standards of caring for our grown daughters and, therefore, he should date. *Could I make it all the way to the ashram? Could I psychologically handle what I saw or learned?*

Again, the encouragement of family and friends propped me up from all directions. Eric handled my emotional turmoil with patience and grace. As the time drew closer to our departure, I gritted my teeth and adopted the adage, "When you fall off a horse, you have to get back on." There was nothing else for it.

The day before leaving, an idea popped into my head. I cut more rectangles of rainbow-colored scraps from damaged dresses donated to Dress for a Good Cause and tossed them into my luggage. Next to them, I threw in a line of twine and a permanent marker.

Chapter 17—On the Road

Arriving at the girls' shelter in the eastern Indian state of Bihar was no easy feat, but the two-day grueling trek from my closest airport to the door of the center's guest cottage was nothing if not fascinating. From the plane window, we saw snow-capped Himalayas that poked through puffy white clouds. At the airport, Mike, Kathryn, and I piled into a large car with Supriya, whose vision helped create the rehabilitation center and whose competence helps maintain it. An Indian driver who was an expert at darting around vehicles sped us away from heavily populated areas into the countryside. We passed fields of tea—rows of low green bushes topped with spring-green leaves ready to be plucked and boiled to fill china cups throughout the world.

As we drove, Supriya's commentary and the sights from the safety of our car underscored the purpose of our visit. Her explanations of things we saw emphasized the urgency and necessity of the work of Free the Slaves, International Justice Mission, and other antislavery groups. Odds were high that the people we saw harvesting leaves in the distance of the tea gardens were bonded laborers—families whose ancestors had traded labor to pay off debt, which was calculated to never end because of interest or other schemes. Most likely, trees planted at regular intervals along the rows were there to provide shade for the tea bushes, *not* humans working the fields. Chimneys from brick factories that operate on the backs of slaves dotted the horizon.

Passing through an intersection that served as a truck stop, we saw young girls—minors—waiting for traffickers, pimps, johns, and middlemen to determine their future, horrific in too many cases. When they caught sight of my camera lens poking above the level of the car window, the girls ran for cover. Men who appeared as though they were standing at a kiosk to purchase soda and chips shot me dirty looks. Supriya explained that the facade of the booth for refreshments or sundries was nothing more than a front for the sex trade. She urged me to take photos a bit more quickly, and our car accelerated past the intersection and down the road.

As the sun set, we crawled through an overcrowded town crammed with congested foot and vehicle traffic, tiny shops, and multistory buildings with exposed nests of electrical wires on upper-story wooden balconies and eaves. In near pitch-black darkness we passed villages without electricity or streetlights. Tiny candles or miniscule oil lamps occasionally lit faces of villagers outside a one-room home with mud walls and a thatched roof.

At the end of the bumpiest, most washboard-like road I had ever traveled and far beyond consistent electrical power, tall solar streetlamps—recently provided by Mark Little and his fellow Rotarians—shined brightly in the foggy night. Like beacons, they welcomed us to Punarnawa Ashram.

Supriya introduced us to Amita, a beautiful, cheery young woman in charge of daily operations at the ashram. She also introduced us to a few of the residents—girls who were quiet and observant, one who was withdrawn and deeply sad, and a youngster who fairly danced around Supriya with excitement. Now late at night, we were ravenous and eagerly kicked off our sandals to enter the kitchen for a superb supper of fresh lentils, vegetables, and fragrant, warm, homemade bread.

When we were warm and full, Mike departed with the driver to find lodging at the closest town since male visitors were not allowed to stay overnight on the premises. Supriya, Kathryn, and I headed into the cozy, simple guest quarters on the property.

My head was a jumble of thoughts as I crawled into a sleeping bag liner with built-in insect repellant to discourage mosquitoes with malaria from joining me in bed. It had taken two full days to travel to this destination. But it had taken two full years for my body to arrive at my heart's desire. Drifting off to sleep I realized I had made it.

Chapter 18—Beginning Anew

Not yet adjusted to the ten-and-a-half-hour time zone difference between Pennsylvania and Bihar, I woke long before sunrise. I was also excited—ready to see the campus in daylight, to learn about Punarnawa's daily routines, and to visit the girls. At the first hint of dawn I dressed, wrapped a shawl around my shoulders, and took my camera on a walk around the grounds, quiet except for the coo of mourning doves.

Unnoticed in the misty darkness of the previous night, a huge, well-tended garden encircled the little yellow guest cottage. It was bursting with flowers—tall bushes of sunshine-yellow and deep orange marigolds, scarlet canna, peach-colored celosia, and two papaya trees heavy with fruit. My camera clicked away. I also snapped photos of flowers unknown to my Pennsylvania garden—magenta blossoms I'd never seen before and cheery blooms with yellow faces and ruffled white petals.

In the center of the garden, a low unpretentious monument stood in dedication to Sant Kabir Math, the foundation that donated the land for the center. Carefully manicured tufts of green grass spelled out against the red earth, "Welcome to Punarnawa." Welcome to New Beginnings.

Surveying a field of yellow lentils, a row of turmeric spice plants, a plot of recently tilled ground, and other gardens around the property, I discovered I was not the only one up and moving. Next to a water pump, two girls watched my activities. I wandered over to them.

It seemed that the morning routine had been quietly in progress for a while. Many girls had risen in time for dawn prayers, each following her personal faith. Some practiced yoga. They began early chores, including pumping water from a well to wash their clothes as well as themselves.

Within moments a few more girls, draped in wool to keep out the chilly morning air, shyly approached us. Amita, the cheerful coordinator, appeared as if by magic and began to translate morning greetings from English to Hindi and back. I turned my camera around to show them the images of their gardens and share my love of flowers. With that the girls warmed to me and led me to a small outdoor temple they had created in the backyard behind the kitchen. Deep purple blossoms of butterfly pea vines blanketed a tiny altar. The girls waited with anticipation for me to take close-up shots of the violet blooms and to reveal the instant images on the little screen.

They pointed out additional objects for me to photograph and clamored to see the results. They implored me to take a picture of a bird that hopped in the grass next to the pump. They squealed when it flew several feet away and, like the paparazzi and zealous fans, we followed it between the clusters of little buildings and around the yard.

Across the grounds, a cow grazed in the grass. *Could this be one of the cows donated by my friends?* It seemed likely, and I smiled at the thought.

My daughter Kathryn showed up at my side. Our minds running on the same track, wordlessly we walked together toward the small brown-and-white, four-legged creature that wore a red, yellow, and green halter. It was tethered to a post. Amita and one girl continued with us to visit the cows in the cowshed while the rest of the group resumed their regular schedules at different parts of the campus. The girl who joined us, we learned, had taken an interest in animal husbandry as a means of supporting herself after she was ready to leave Punarnawa.

Morning tasks included "feeding" the bio-gas system. Kathryn and I watched the process. After my mini-study of manure, digesters, and methane, I wasn't disappointed seeing it in action. Amita picked up dry dung cakes from the ground around the shed and piled them into a plastic bucket. Surprisingly they had no smell. When the bucket was full, a young man from the village—staying well away from any of the girls for the sake of their privacy and protection, as was the policy for any male visiting the center—carried the bucket on top of his head across the campus. He deposited the bucket next to a circular concrete container with a small hole in the bottom. Then he stepped back while Amita loaded the dung from the bucket into the bottom of the round, walled structure. Afterward, he took the empty bucket and walked back to the shed. When he returned, he poured clear liquid—cow urine collected via a channel in the edge of the floor around the cowshed, Amita explained—over the dung. With a hose, she added water to the container. Then she turned a crank that churned the mixture into the consistency of mud and watched as the soupy mess drained below ground via the hole in the bottom of the little tank.

In the underground digester, the manure mixture decomposes, she continued. Methane rises to the top where it travels through a valved pipe to the kitchen and serves as fuel for the stove. She pointed to the pipe, the valve, and the small hole in the back wall of the kitchen where the pipe led to the burners.

We walked several more feet along the back of the building, past the girls' small altar, and to a shallow ditch. From a larger pipe, the muddy mixture minus methane gas drained into the ditch, where it was then collected and used for fertilizing their crops: lentils, potatoes, spices, and fruits.

Later we observed extra hands from the village milk the three cows in the shed. Streams of white liquid squirted into metal buckets. When the pails were full and removed from below the belly of the animals, the three calves were no longer restrained. They rushed to their mothers to nurse. While the calves fed, they were licked by their mothers' long tongues.

After we finished our tour of the bio-gas system, we rounded the building and poked our heads inside the open kitchen door. Girls crouched in a circle on the floor, happily kneading dough, rolling balls of it in their hands, flattening them with a short rolling pin, and placing the perfect circles on a shiny metal plate. The cook, an older woman, pushed a dozen bangles above each wrist as she stirred the steaming contents of large pots and pans on burners.

Methane at work, I marveled. Because of the bio-gas system we had just witnessed, today's breakfast would not need to be cooked over a wood or charcoal fire. Meals wouldn't rely on an electric stove that would be out of commission during daily power outages or when a generator wasn't operating. No longer would the ashram bear the expense of canisters of cooking fuel.

Kathryn washed her hands and bent down to join the circle. Within moments she had settled into the group to help knead *naan*—the flatbread for our breakfast. I left Kathryn and the other girls in the kitchen, where the small round dough balls increased in number and the stack of flattened naan grew, when Amita announced that my bathwater was nearly hot.

By the time I arrived back at the little guest cottage, Amita had left a bucket of steaming bathwater at my door. I carried it into the bathroom and proceeded with my bath. In a second large bucket I mixed cold tap water and the scalding water with the aid of a small plastic pitcher as ladle and stirrer. When the water temperature was perfect, I knelt between the bucket and the drain in the floor, now using the small pitcher to pour fresh warm water over my hair and back.

Accustomed to standing beneath a showerhead, my usual choreography was useless. My new sequence of motions— dip water, stand up, lather up, rinse with clean water, avoid mixing soapy water with fresh, kneel—felt clumsy. Used to a glass door or shower curtain to contain any splashes of water, I created a small swimming pool in the open layout of the tiled room. From the corner where I bathed to the center of the room where the toilet sat on a raised block, the bathroom looked like a three-year-old had unleashed a flood. Snickering, it took me as long to tidy up my mess, as it had to wash myself.

Clean again, I slipped into a fresh *salwar kameez*—a long, flowing tunic of amethyst and emerald, with matching silky scarf and loose-fitting trousers of green—and comfortable sandals. I pulled my hair into a knot at the back of my head in preparation of the day's upcoming heat and in a nod to Indian fashion.

Then I headed into the yard again. There, I found Supriya talking with the ashram's guards on the day shift. Her energy was palpable even several feet away—she could participate in a rescue on one side of the globe one week and then solicit help from and update the center's donors in the States the following week. It was not out of the ordinary for her to juggle meetings with visitors from another country's state department, a survivor's lawyer, or staff members needing help with a budget or to contemplate types of crops to plant after staying up half the night providing comfort to a distraught survivor.

Supriya and I ambled to the kitchen and picked up mugs of delectable fresh chai, sugar, and milk fresh from the cow. Cups in hand, Kathryn joined us to walk around the yard. We shed our shawls as the temperature climbed and the dazzling sun burned off any lingering wisps of fog.

Supriya introduced us to girls who chattered happily between morning tasks. One was Jaya,* a graduate of the program who had returned to Punarnawa to learn additional sewing techniques from the ashram's teachers. Successfully reintegrated into her village, her tailoring business was thriving and she was ready to expand it. It was easy to see that her presence would be an inspiration to other girls at the ashram and in her village. Her composure and self-esteem were regal. Her twinkling eyes and warm smile were joyous. Her bubbling laughter rippled through the group of us who had gathered by her dorm. When

Jaya excused herself to pack for the trip back to her village for a religious festival, I was already looking forward to visiting her in her home and at her shop—the next day's trip as promised by Supriya.

Chapter 19—Lessons

That morning Supriya, Kathryn, and I greeted Mike when he arrived at the gate and then continued our stroll throughout the property. Every few steps we encountered something new to learn about the ashram. Rows of red buckets filled with water and sand hung outside each building. Previously they were the only "sprinkler system" until enough cylindrical modern fire extinguishers could be located and purchased; they were now kept as a back-up fire system. A yellow kitten, adopted by the ashram's residents, paid us a visit and then stretched out lazily on a shady porch. A dog—once hoped to serve as a guard and warning system, but found to be too curious and friendly to become a traditional watchdog, Supriya explained—trotted behind us.

Mike, Kathryn, and I met the milkman who came to Punarnawa's entrance. He collected large buckets of extra milk to be sold at the nearby market. I watched him ride down the washboard road on his old bicycle, a large metal canister of milk on each side of the back wheel and artificial flowers adorning the handlebars.

Adhering to the ashram's strict policy of no male contact with the survivors, Mike separated from Kathryn and me for further exploration and education about the center. Investigating his areas of expertise—practical matters of projects such as financing, building, and problem solving—Mike headed to the business office, outlying corners of the property, and site of the pavilion construction. Kathryn headed to the freshly tilled field and grabbed a handful of dirt to inspect it before catching up with me again.

She and I marched off to school, where the girls were already deep into their studies in the privacy of their classroom. We passed workers from the adjacent village, allowed into the compound to construct a pavilion funded by several Rotarians and their clubs. Some wearing Western-style trousers and others wearing traditional *dhoties*—fabric tied skirt-like around the waist—the men hoisted and carried buckets of gravel on their heads and pounded iron bars to form supports for columns.

Entering the small schoolroom was like crossing a threshold into another garden. Dressed in salwar kameez outfits of fuchsia, marigold, rose, and leaf-green, ten young girls sat in rows behind low desks on woven rugs covering the floor. Heads bent low over a math assignment, they looked up in synchrony, like flower buds blowing in a mild breeze, when a lovely young teacher and Amita invited us into the room.

Reminiscent of my early visit to the survivors' home in Pennsylvania, I presented children's picture books to the teacher. She handed one to each girl, carefully selecting a book that matched the student's reading level and English comprehension.

After the girls read their original books and traded for others, the teacher chose one to read aloud with the group. "I see two pink flowers," she read. "I see two ..."

"Two yellow flowers," the students chorused. For an instant I was transported back in time to the afternoon I first met Ati, Nadira, and Narbelung, survivors of international human trafficking who were learning English and recovering near my home.

Delighted by a colorful poster on the classroom wall, I took a picture of it. The girls—the artists who had drawn the collaborative work—were overjoyed. Once again, the click of the camera led the way with rapport. Nine of the girls jostled against my elbow with coloring books, sketch pads, and math papers. Page by page, they held their work in front of the lens and then checked the digital screen to ensure that their offerings had been clearly captured. They smiled to see their work so admired.

One smaller but older girl participated in the lessons at her desk yet remained disconnected from the group's interactions. We had seen each other soon after my nighttime arrival to the center, but I had a better opportunity in daylight to observe her countenance. She made little eye contact and rarely spoke. The other girls placed her drawings and math homework in front of my camera to make certain she was included, but she remained reclusive at her corner desk. I sat on the floor next to her and showed her the images of her work. She looked at my face for a moment and concentrated for a few minutes on the camera screen, but she never uttered a word or changed her distant, serious expression. I could scarcely imagine the life she had experienced before she reached this little classroom at Punarnawa.

Chapter 20—New Directions

The clear tinkle of a brass bell turned me toward the kitchen. Lunch was ready. It was time to pick up a plate of aromatic rice, carrots, onions, and lentils—delicious sustenance for me and a helping of comfort for others at the ashram.

I have always felt that food and spirituality are connected at a very deep level. To nourish the body with wholesome, lovingly prepared food is to nurture the soul. To serve my family homemade pasta, basil, and tomatoes from my own garden, berries gathered from behind our Quaker meetinghouse, and honey carefully collected by my friend Jan who keeps bees is an act of grace. To gather the family around the table over a meal is the most basic foundation of life.

My understanding of the role of food as a manifestation of love grew as I viewed the world from the eyes of survivors. Smells, flavors, and textures of food eaten during childhood signify home and places and people to which we belong. As crawling babies, we come to know even the color of the soil in which the food of our homeland grows. Even before we develop language to express the knowledge, we are familiar with the dirt—rust-colored in Bihar, milk-chocolate brown in Pennsylvania—that is washed from our homegrown root vegetables.

To be deprived of comfort food—enough food and meals that taste familiar and nurture our bodies and hearts—is to steal our sense of belonging. Was it any wonder then that the boys at Bal Vikas Ashram ate mounds of rice? Was it any revelation that Ati, Nadira, and Narbelung would boil strange-looking vegetables, prepare unidentifiable dishes—odd green semicircles with fiery-looking orange flecks on top—and feed the Circle of Friends fresh Asian dumplings? Beyond food's properties to help mend physical ailments, it healed emotional wounds.

With lunch finished and the sun high in the sky, we moved to the next activities of the day. Afternoons at Punarnawa looked to another aspect of the residents' future—job training and self-sufficiency. The cycle of extreme poverty and lack of options that had led to the girls' victimization needed to be reversed.

In addition to their academic studies, teens at the ashram learned trades that would help support them after reintegration into their families and villages. They made candles—colorful wax roses and birds sprinkled with a hint of glitter—that would be found in family altars or on tables in homes without consistent electricity. They learned to farm with simple hand-held tools. Girls practiced skills to become tailors on colorful sewing machines with foot-powered treadles.

The tools the girls used at the center would go home with them to help them begin their own businesses, Supriya explained. Each and every girl was bright enough to drive a tractor or employ sophisticated power tools, but odds were slim that a village that could barely afford food would own a tractor or that the girls would return to homes and workplaces with reliable electrical power.

While the teens continued their vocational training, Kathryn and I left the tool shed and crossed the yard to join the younger girls in a cheerful yet plain multipurpose room. We spread a large, thick, woven blanket on the floor, and I placed a rainbow of embroidery floss in the center. Half a dozen girls, a teacher, Kathryn, and I formed a circle on the rug. I selected strands of three colors, fastened them with a loop and a knot at one end, and hooked the loop around my toe. I began to braid the long strands. Kathryn and I next offered threads to our fellow group members. Her youth and natural ease in interacting with people drew onlookers into the activity.

Bashfully at first and then more boldly, girls requested blue, pink, and orange threads that had formed a tangled nest in my backpack. The girls were quiet and focused as they deftly untangled filaments and braided them into colorful strings. They easily mimicked Kathryn's movements to weave more complex patterns. Within moments they tied pretty bracelets around their wrists and ankles. I slipped the one I created around the wrist of the little girl sitting next to me in the circle. Pavitra* attached the ends of hers around my arm, where it now stays.

I reflected on our activity. To some people, traveling thousands of miles to make bracelets might seem like a trivial pastime. In reality, it was serious business that accompanied the vital help that money supplied—dairy products, lamps, fuel, a roof. Making bracelets provided a connection among females who don't share a common language but wanted to show they care. It helped girls learn to play again. It was the type of interaction that children deserve to enjoy. Such moments only magnified for me the ever-present monster of child slavery and the despicable acts of sex traffickers who preyed on innocence.

At the end of our activity, we tidied the floor together, picking up bits of colored thread. Kathryn, the teacher, and I folded the blanket and placed it on a counter along a side wall. Before closing the door to the room, I took one more look around to make sure that all was in order. A photo of Mahatma Gandhi smiled down at me from a spot near the ceiling.

Chapter 21—Monsters at Night

Why do monsters come out at night? Does sunshine chase them away? Or are they always with us—day and night—but moonlight makes them visible? Maybe our minds and hands are just too busy during the day to allow them to intrude on our thoughts. In the quiet of the night, the girls' stories—learned during daylight—took a new, larger, more hideous form.

The girls were flung into sex slavery by kidnapping and trickery … even by being sold to human devils by villainous distant relatives. Many had been deceived—promised an education in return for minimal hours of light work—but were delivered instead into an existence of exploitation, confinement, and terror. They were children, some as young as seven, yet they had already seen the horrors of brothels, truck stops, and homes of well-to-do bureaucrats. Some were rescued in transit; others spent years in places where numerous men daily and nightly paid slaveholders to abuse them. They came to Punarnawa from Katmandu, the red-light districts of Delhi, Mumbai, and elsewhere.

One little girl had been saved because of a customer. Distraught, she told him that she had been abducted earlier that day and gave him her sister's cell phone number. After leaving the bordello, the customer called the sister and reported the girl's location. The sister immediately notified authorities. The child was rescued that day, but only after five customers had raped her.

Her story broke my heart. It also perplexed me. A customer, whose demand for sex was partially responsible for her captivity, was also partially responsible for her rescue. What made him draw the line to help instead of harm her, while he seemingly easily crossed other lines? Did he fool himself into thinking that females would choose to entertain ten men per day every single day of the week? Couldn't he guess what pain or diseases would be the consequences? I felt sickened at the thought.

Aanisah,* unsure of her exact age, was rescued at eighteen or nineteen years old after being sold into a brothel five years earlier. Like many girls in her situation, she was ashamed to return home, although she was blameless. Aanisah was so afraid that her family and villagers would no longer accept her that she fastidiously guarded the name of her home village. Consequently, social workers could not discover her past and try to build bridges for her return.

Aditi* was taken at such a young age to Katmandu by an uncle, who sold her as a domestic worker, that when she was found by police years later she had forgotten the name of her hometown. She could no longer remember her native language.

For a long time that night I lay awake in the dark with my eyes closed. Visions and thoughts from the day tangled with strings of previous memories and conversations—with Maina, Mark, rape victims, and detectives in police stations, college professors, and the liberators of children and adults from captivity. I recalled journalists Ben Skinner's and Nicholas Kristof's accounts of girls who endure torture when they resist sex or attempt escape. I felt disgusted and horrified. I loathed the perpetrators of vile acts.

If not for the solar streetlamps shining through the guest house windows and the sound of Kathryn's breathing, the monsters might have loomed even larger in my mind.

Chapter 22—Growing Concerns

More strands of memories and disturbing conversations snaked their way into the messy knot in my brain. Statistics and facts extracted from a seminar provided an academic frame around the human faces I had seen and the stories I had heard during daytime.

"It is as easy for traffickers transporting thirteen-year-old Latvian girls to pass the borders of Germany, the Netherlands, and other European nations as it is for vacation travelers to cross US state lines from Pennsylvania to New York," Dr. Mark Rodgers had said at a spring 2011 seminar. The guest lecturer—dean of the Graduate School of Social Work at Dominican University and a member of the Chicago-based Taskforce on Human Trafficking—had helped form antitrafficking programs and policies in Latvia and Ecuador.

Could Isaac Newton have foreseen such implications of his law—that every action has an equal yet opposite reaction—on progress and slavery? When Latvia became a member of the European Union in 2004, it entered a sophisticated modern economy and provided citizens with opportunities for prosperity, justice, and democracy. The reaction—giving criminals opportunities for injustice and tyranny—was created also. Like many other nations, Latvia was classified by the US State Department as a recruitment, transit, and destination nation, for human trafficking victims.

Rodgers's lecture had provided other shocking facts:

- Profits from *human* trafficking, second only to *drug* trafficking, were expected to surpass that of the drug trade within a few years.
- Child trafficking and sexual exploitation were on the rise.
- Victims of the forced sex trade were becoming younger because offending "consumers" believe their risk for HIV/AIDS is lower with youngsters, and because child pornography and sex tourism were expanding. A law enforcement study in Chicago found that the average age of entry into the commercial sexual exploitation of children was between thirteen and a half and fourteen.
- International children trafficked into the United States and other developed nations often progress from forced labor to the forced sex trade. They are bought and sold several times, viewed as a cheap and disposable commodity. Hundreds of thousands of children are bought and sold, forced to trade sex with numerous men each night, beaten and humiliated and sometimes killed, according to End Child Prostitution and Trafficking (ECPAT-USA).

Another conversation at a restaurant a few days before my trip to Punarnawa played back in my mind. It underscored the complexities and horrors inflicted by ruthless perpetrators on victims and people with solid morals and deep conscience.

My friend Bob told me that a decade earlier, he had traveled to China for business. After a long day of work, he accepted his Chinese business hosts' invitation to dinner and a nightcap at a karaoke bar. After their meal, the men were ushered into a private room where beautiful young women, in addition to a karaoke machine, entertained them. It became apparent that Bob was expected to take one of the females back to his hotel bedroom. After an extended period at the microphone and a distraught long-distance call to his wife from the restaurant's men's room, Bob explained his principles to his hosts and to an intense, agitated female maitre d'.

He left the party alone but with a great weight on his mind: What would become of the girl he had turned down? Would she suffer at the hands of her "employers" because they blamed her for displeasing him or because she did not deliver a product for a price already paid?

Years later, Bob began an antislavery group within the Religious Society of Friends and became an early member of a coalition against human trafficking in his county. But his experience and his concern for the girl continued to haunt him.

Chapter 23—Where No Man Can Go

When your body is the scene of the crime, where do you go to escape it?

For the girls at the ashram, and for any rape or abuse victim, female or male, there is nowhere on earth they can leave behind, even for a moment, the crime scene and evidence of harm. We humans *are* our bodies, integrated with our hearts, souls, and minds. Consequently, even the most loving touch can be a reminder of pain. For many girls at Punarnawa and elsewhere, the mere presence of a man brings back trauma. Even the male calf at the ashram was deemed by residents to be the first sold when it was time.

There are, however, two places where female victims can go to find healing and peace. They are places where no man can go: inside shelters like Punarnawa and the survivors' residence in Pennsylvania, and deep inside a quiet corner in a female's own mind. Both can be safe havens.

At the centers for female survivors, caring male rescuers sometimes bring women to the gate. Dedicated, concerned men serve as guards at the border of Punarnawa's property; a male accountant ensures that bills are paid. But no man enters the dormitories and spaces where the girls or women gather. Even Mike, who accompanied Kathryn and me on a ten-thousand-mile journey to this remote area, stayed at a nearby inn. While Kathryn and I interacted with girls, he remained respectfully at a distance and visited other areas of the campus.

Most people I know have a little cave or "happy place" in a corner of their mind. A mental space for imagination, dreams, fantasy, or refuge, it is a room to retreat for processing the day's events or escaping them. For some victims, mental escapes go too far. Dissociation—a state of consciousness in which a person is so detached from his or her emotions and surroundings that he or she cannot function normally—must be dealt with in therapy, at the same time the original trauma is addressed. When done in a healthy way, however, meditation, prayer, or reflection to reach a tranquil inner harbor is a way to soothe jangled nerves before choosing to return to a safe space in the present.

Still awake in my sleeping bag liner in the ashram's guest room, I considered the contradictions of language. Is being rescued from slavery a wonderful thing? Is being a former slave a horrible thing? I pondered questions I could not answer. Does better physical health make emotional scars more vivid and nightmarish memories stronger? At children's ashrams, do beautiful faces and smiles mask the atrocities that have occurred? Is the relief and joy of freedom real? Do the singing and laughter during chores, the perfume of incense from morning meditation, and the beauty of the tropical garden lull me into false contentment? If the human memory is still intact, can paradise exist after emerging from hell?

How can we figure out how to help when every mention or question about a crime retraumatizes its victim? What could any one of us say to a person who has been brutally harmed by another human? I remembered the answer to that last question, one of my greatest lessons from the Crime Victims' Center: Nothing, at first, can be said. More important than any words is the gift of listening—hearing with the heart and both ears.

Eventually, the swirl in my mind left me alone long enough to fall asleep for a few hours.

*

Awake again at 4:00 a.m. and unable to fall back asleep, I crawled out of bed. I crept silently to the back of the kitchen and Punarnawa's little temple. The night was damp from fog, and scores of flowers appeared pale in the diffused light of the nearly full moon. I was alone with the small figures of the gods Ganesha and Vishnu, stubs of incense sticks, and the previous day's garland of orange marigolds. Even the ashram's dog had chosen to stay sleeping at my front door rather than follow me to the tiny place of worship.

Unexpectedly, tears washed down my face in sheets. They were as quiet as the night, and I fought to keep my breathing silent so the girls in the dorm just feet away didn't wake to any noise. When tears had made my lips salty and reached my chin, I wiped them away with my sleeve. I hurt for these children at a depth and breadth that could not be measured. How many tears would have to be shed—by the parents and loved ones of victims, the caregivers and healers of survivors, people whose souls refused to become numb, and by slaves themselves—before we figure out a true solution to end them?

Crying, I prayed to Ganesha, the Hindu god who removes obstacles, to help me keep my promise made after meeting Maina—to help the victims of slavery, those who are rescued and those who are still in bondage. I asked for help to overcome whatever challenges lay ahead as I wrote about the monster of child slavery and sought aid to help survivors.

Someone else's call to prayer was the first sound to break the night's silence. First one voice from a seemingly distant hamlet, and then another from a different direction, and then another seemed to float from a nearby mosque. The voices were mournful and hopeful all at once. Next came a small chorus of chattering birds and the lone bark of a dog. Only as the chorus of birds rose did the rooster crow.

Slowly, slowly, the sky brightened. The haze changed from pale gold of sunrise to the gray and white of morning. I slowly walked back to my room.

At breakfast we learned the news that during the night, another girl had been rescued and brought to the center.

Chapter 24—Victory

Jaya met us at the entrance of her village. Jaya's family, friends, close relatives, and more distant relatives crowded around her and peeked into our car windows before our car doors opened. For us to climb out of our vehicle, curious onlookers had to make a space to let us out. Led by Jaya and trailed by a small crowd, Mike, Kathryn, Supriya, and I crossed a tidy, swept dirt courtyard past bamboo trees, palms, and mud and thatch homes to Jaya's tailoring business and her little room.

A ten-foot-square space served as her bedroom, garage for her bicycle, storage for onions, sitting room for welcoming us, and headquarters for her thriving enterprises. The view from her glass-less windows included her parents' room opposite a wall and green bamboo trees and bamboo-grid fencing on the other side of an outside wall. Her thick, unfinished wooden door was bolted with a heavy wrought iron latch and further secured with a sturdy wooden pole wedged between the latch and the dirt floor. A single bare bulb below the thatched roof shed light on a wall covered in colorful posters, typical decoration for a teenage girl. Yet there was nothing typical about Jaya or her story.

At sixteen, Jaya had been abducted one day when her father was working in Nepal, struggling to earn a living to feed a family in a village rife with poverty. After two days of being locked in a room, she escaped before her trafficker delivered her to a brothel.

She spent nine months at Punarnawa, expanding her academic and vocational education, a rare occurrence for females in her region. She learned about human rights and causes of slavery, eventually understanding her previous vulnerabilities that had led to her trafficking. She developed self-confidence and decided to pursue a legal case against her trafficker, despite social norms and intense pressure from the trafficker's family members for her to remain silent.

When a local partner of Free the Slaves had determined that her family's financial situation was stable and the village was safe, Jaya returned home and put to use the tailoring practices she learned at Punarnawa. She taught other village girls how to sew, bought a tailoring business, became the first female tailor in the village, and built a substantial livelihood. With some of her profits, she bought unprocessed rice. Then she processed it and sold it at a higher price on the market. With that profit, the seventeen-year-old invested in better seed and fertilizer to improve the farmer's crop and increase the yield, ensuring she had a better product to work with.

Not long after she had been home, an unexpected event solidified her resolve to speak out, protect other girls, and make change. When another local girl was trafficked the same way she had been, she notified antislavery workers. The girl was rescued and taken to Punarnawa. Jaya and the other girl pursued justice and testified against the perpetrator. The trafficker was locked behind bars.

Jaya beckoned to us to join her on a walk through the village. She took Kathryn by the hand and led us down a narrow path past huts and a cow drinking water from a trough. She stopped at a cluster of trees between the village homes and a large field bisected by a dirt path that led to a modern highway.

"This is where it happened," Jaya said without drama. She observed the spot where her kidnapper had thrown a cloth over her head before dragging her across the field and shoving her into a vehicle at the highway.

She looked from the throng of villagers, including some of the family members of her trafficker who had followed us, to our trio of Americans, Supriya, and her other advocates from Free the Slaves. Her eyes sent a resounding message through the crowd. Jaya had retaken control of her life, power, and the path we had just walked; the sale and sexual exploitation of girls would not take place in the village again. As witnessed by Americans— Kathryn, Mike, and me, from thousands of miles away—she informed the village that it was no longer isolated. The eyes of the world were upon it.

Chapter 25—A Pound of Prevention

Supriya, Free the Slaves' partners, Kathryn, Mike, and I spent the rest of a long day making field visits to various far-flung villages. We met boys who had been reunited with their families after being enslaved and treated at Bal Vikas Ashram, where Mark, Mike, and I had visited the previous year. Our travels took us past fields where workers bundled jute to become the backs of rugs, rice grew, and families camped under tents of tattered tarps and cloth.

Our little band checked in on another graduate of Punarnawa, another girl who recently set up a tailoring business and was at home again with her family. The closest thing to privacy in a crowded village setting, Mike, Kathryn, and I distracted the family in a conversation about the shop long enough for Supriya to hold a quick, whispered conversation with Punarnawa's graduate. She sought candid answers to important questions about the girl's readjustment and sense of security.

At one stop, we sat cross-legged on the shady ground at a community vigilance meeting at a remote hamlet of India near the borders of Nepal and Bangladesh. Villagers stood under the eaves of thatched roofs or bamboo trees to watch the meeting over the heads of the men who sat with us on mats. Women with babies, children, and teenage boys observed and listened closely to the proceedings, all very quiet except for an old man who belched regularly and loudly. Two boys joined the grown men on the ground.

Supriya translated and explained the meeting's business. Free the Slaves' educators and an established community vigilance committee from a nearby hamlet had stepped in after two twelve-year-old boys from this Hindu community's hamlet were trafficked with five other local boys the previous year. The boys—the ones with us in the gathering—were rescued before they had reached their intended work site in Delhi. They received help at Bal Vikas Ashram and returned home.

The educators and concerned citizens from the neighboring village began to teach the villagers how to further protect children from slavery and inform them of their human rights.

With nearly no access to schooling, and freedom not guaranteed in the region, the villagers did not know that liberty is every human's right. They had no clue that the government had granted them rights to the land they and their ancestors had occupied. In such a meeting as the one we attended—large circles of families gathered in the humblest of settings, without benches, whiteboards, slide presentations, handouts, or refreshments— they learned from Free the Slaves' workers and their neighbors that children's education is free and compulsory by law and that citizens are entitled to converse with elected leaders.

The man who headed the other village's committee spoke. His son had been trafficked and rescued a few years earlier. Knowing firsthand the heartache of nearly losing a child, the father helped his own village committee become strong to guard its community members and then sought to help nearby communities learn to protect themselves.

Since the educators and other villagers' committee had been working with the new committee in the hamlet, not a single child had been trafficked. Families without food and out of work, in a village that already existed well below the poverty line, were getting assistance with food and finding access to health care. Villagers were becoming aware, educated, and less vulnerable. Change was taking hold.

Miles away from our morning location with further visits to reintegrated survivors accomplished, we grabbed an odd assortment of Asian and Western foods for supper at a gas station and headed back. Well into the night we arrived back at Punarnawa's gate, where the nighttime security guards let us in.

Chapter 26—Finding Hope

I didn't notice the exact point when Kathryn and I had been incorporated into the ashram's morning routines or when we had become accepted, familiar members of Punarnawa's extended family. But by our last breakfast together, the girls comfortably called us *didi*—"elder sister"—and kept us company as we walked about the little campus.

On the final day of our visit to the ashram, I pulled the colorful fabric scraps of Dress for a Good Cause castoffs, permanent marker, and twine from my suitcase. I stuffed them into my camera case. Kathryn and I wandered to the youngest girls' dormitory. A *rangoli*—a beautiful colored-chalk design drawn "to please God," as the word rangoli translates literally—on the floor of the porch greeted us. The stylized artwork depicting pink and white flower petals and leaves transformed the ordinary concrete into a charming path.

Two girls showed us the bright yellow marigolds they planted next to the large porch. They cupped their small hands around the perfect blooms so I could take another series of pictures of their handiwork. I thought about the act of sowing seeds, nurturing seedlings, and waiting for buds. Creating a space that is beautiful, doing something that creates a future is an act that occurs only when there is hope. I wondered if I had ever encountered a place so filled with hope and promise as Punarnawa Ashram.

While I reviewed my photos, the quiet girl who was so withdrawn rested her head against my arm. It was a rare moment of connection with a child who seemed mentally so far away. Without saying a word she watched the pictures appear one-by-one on the screen.

A dozen girls joined us on the dorm porch. I dumped the fabric, twine, and permanent pen from a pocket in my camera bag onto a table. Then I strung the twine from a porch column to a metal piece on a low window frame.

On a scrap of pale blue satin, I wrote my deepest wish for the ashram: *serenity to the souls who walk its grounds and the soles that touch its earth.* Then I tied the little flag to the twine. Kathryn and Supriya chose pretty scraps, added their hopes, and hung them on the line. Soon all the girls and several staff members were selecting bits of favorite colors and waiting to write with the marker. Even the most solitary girl added her offering.

They told us the dreams written in Hindi and English on their banners: "To be a doctor," and "To be with my mom and dad soon." A pink banner said simply, "I love you, God." Another girl whose native northern Indian language was different from that of the others drew a flower on a scrap of yellow silk. The wishes hung like Nepalese prayer flags—pink, lavender, red, lime-green, yellow, silver, and blue—above their garden of marigolds and in the dazzling sunshine.

In the background, a mural painted by survivors and volunteers spread across the front of the dormitory. At the center, symbols of Hindu, Christian, and Muslim faiths graced the walls and told newcomers that all were welcome. Aspects of their lives were depicted in brilliant colors: bicycles, flowers of red and blue, little houses, brown and orange goats, and green parrots.

The mural revealed feelings: tears on one face, smiles on others. One stick figure revealed possibilities for future love and marriage—a cartoonish smiling stick figure with a fancy hairdo and an earring facing a stick figure wearing trousers, with three red hearts between their faces.

The self-portraits were a window into their identities, perspectives, and dreams. The survivors had painted themselves as stick figures or drawn childlike renditions of bodies with long black hair, dark eyes, and red lips; many showed chandelier earrings. One wore a red sari. One, in an outfit that resembled a school uniform, stood in front of a chalkboard filled with ABCs and next to a sewing machine. They showed their activities—sewing, riding bikes, eating, holding hands with girlfriends. The simple drawings depicted the journey away from captivity and a life without a voice into a future brimming with possibilities, self-esteem, self-expression, and power to pursue a life of one's choosing.

I was struck by the writing at the very top of the mural, a question posed by Robert Schuller and introduced to me on a card from my husband years ago. The question touched the minds and hearts of Punarnawa's residents and visitors alike: "What would you attempt to do if you knew you could not fail?"

If I knew I could abolish slavery, what action would I take? If I could save the life of one girl or change the circumstances of twenty-seven million slaves worldwide, would I buy a cup of fair trade coffee, make a donation, teach a child to read, demand a new law, or spread the word that slavery must stop? What would others attempt to do if they knew they could not fail?

There was no doubt of the pain, anguish, fear, and sadness that lived in the hearts of girls in the ashram. As I had learned when volunteering at the Crime Victims' Center near my home, sexual abuse is traumatizing and life-changing. At the same time, the girls at Punarnawa were healing, recovering, and regaining control of their disrupted lives. They were receiving protection, immeasurable love, and meticulous care. The skills they were learning—reading, writing, farming, tailoring, cooking—and the confidence they built were transforming their lives yet again.

In the paintings in the murals, the flowers in the garden, the prayers on the colorful flags, and in the lovely faces of the girls there was the evidence that beyond recovering and surviving was the hope of new beginnings.

Chapter 27—Going Home

How could our time at Punarnawa Ashram have flown by so quickly? I wasn't sure I was ready to leave. I wanted to spend just a few more days or hours to learn more and to become more familiar with newfound friends. Contrary to the previous year's trip when I couldn't get home fast enough and I was truly afraid that I would fly home in a coffin, this year I felt stronger, healthier, and more refreshed than when our vehicle entered the center's gate.

I was ready to see my husband, Eric, and daughter Elizabeth again, to share the triumphs of our trip and to report to friends on the great progress of the donated cows, bio-gas system, and pavilion. I wanted to stay and observe the progress of Aanisah, Aditi, Pavitra, Jaya, Asha and her mouse, and others.

Clichés about home whirled through my mind: home is where the heart is, home is where you hang your hat, a man's home is his castle. I thought about people who had left the home where they were born and created new ones in new lands. Immigrants I knew straddled two families—those of origin and of creation—and two cultures, sets of traditions, and rituals. While it could be said that they had two homes, I wondered in actuality if they had any home at all, short of the head where they hung their hat. Even my mother, raised in one part of the United States and relocated to another as an adult, never really stopped longing for her childhood climate or reminiscing about customs hundreds of miles away.

Maybe the saying "You can't go home again" was the one that was most apt, because, as another adage goes, "You can't step in the same river twice." Life and time move on. We change. Our homes change. I wondered if my town would feel different upon my return. No one would understand this more than girls who prepared for graduation from Punarnawa after enduring experiences that most of us could not bear.

On the way to Bal Vikas Ashram in 2011, the center for boys, Rajneesh—a coordinator and rescuer—had described the phases of recovery and stages of rehabilitation of rescued slaves. Relearning to make choices, to exercise free will, and to live in freedom is an arduous process for people who have learned to survive without freedom or options. In fact, Rajneesh said, for one to three months after being rescued former slaves experience confusion along with relief. Their routines are interrupted. They are in a new, strange environment, and they don't know what rules apply to life.

After a period of adjustment, however, happiness sets in. Survivors' needs are met and they are being cared for. For a time, they are dependent on other people to help them learn skills to deal with a new environment and lifestyle. In final stages of recovery, survivors become self-reliant. Although some survivors will continually struggle, depending on the individual, self-reliance is achieved after a year, possibly two or three.

To work toward the goals of self-reliance, empowerment, and self-sufficiency, rehabilitation takes four stages, continued Rajneesh.

- In the initial stage, survivors are treated for trauma. They receive medical help for any number of problems—malnutrition, undiagnosed or untreated diseases and medical conditions, or untended wounds.
- In the second stage, workers provide them with access to psychological counseling, vocational training, and education. The skills of reading and writing are sometimes achieved in a month, he noted.
- In stage three of rehabilitation, survivors practice activities toward self-reliance. Still under the watchful eye of helpers, they learn to help themselves.
- Finally, corresponding with the phase of self-reliance, survivors are able to help themselves and others. Through careful planning and preparation of family and friends, survivors are reintegrated into village life.

Workers—who, by the final stages, may serve as extended family, friends, and trusted advisers—visit villages to ensure the continued safety and well-being of survivors. As anyone who has been a victim of any crime will attest to, a life derailed by harm takes time to repair. The process of healing might continue for a lifetime, so visits to ensure that survivors' new habits are still holding up serve as a safety net.

Although our time at Punarnawa was short, we had touched the lives of the girls and they had touched ours. Like the strands of our friendship bracelets, our lives were woven together for a short moment in time. Like the braided threads, we seemed stronger, brighter, and more colorful together than when we were separate.

I shoved my luggage—now carrying artwork and candles made by the girls in place of embroidery thread and fabric scraps transformed into crafts left at the center—into the back of our vehicle. Kathryn, Mike, Supriya, and I climbed into our seats. I took one last look at the walls of Punarnawa before bracing myself to head back down the bumpiest road on the planet.

Chapter 28—Afterthoughts

My elevator rides continue downward and upward. The number of travelers who make a conscious decision to descend with me from sunny heights to dark depths in order to help victims seems to be increasing. No trip is more thrilling, however, than the one in which a rescued slave receives an education, trains for a new job, receives her first paycheck, and attains self-sufficiency. It's a slow ride up and it isn't without trepidation, but the view above ground from a survivor's eyes is magnificent.

Despite the inability to find answers to all my questions or solutions to many problems—how consumers can pay to rape a child, how customers can fool themselves into believing that a young girl or boy wants to have sex ten or fifteen times in a night *for money*, and how to uncover beastly crimes that remain hidden—I have found some answers along this journey.

I have also found friends, fellow advocates, abolitionists, and supporters in places I didn't expect. I've learned that the generation of young adults ready to enter the workforce in the next year or two is smart, savvy, more aware of reality, and better equipped to handle challenges of social injustice than older, jaded adults might guess. While there is no time for rest—not while people are still suffering in enslavement—I have found solace in action. I've also found energy to keep hoping and persisting because of the people who lend their moral support, financial contributions, energetic response, and love.

Along the way I have also seen dramatic change and progress. In early 2004, when I returned home after meeting Maina, finding information about human trafficking took effort. The Polaris Project—an organization named after the North Star that guided slaves in America to the region of freedom in the 1800s and fights slavery today—had been founded only two years earlier. Modern pioneers in the field of antislavery, Free the Slaves, in operation since 2000, and the Salvation Army were working hard to get momentum going. Neither Dawn's Place, the residence for female survivors in my area, nor Punarnawa Ashram, for girls in India, existed at the time.

On the contrary, at the beginning of 2012, rarely a week went by when there weren't media reports about the existence of slavery, the mention of a court case involving human traffickers, or a survivor of forced commercial sexual exploitation who came forward to tell her story. New county-level coalitions against human trafficking have sprung up in Pennsylvania and elsewhere. Changes in laws, including passage of an act that requires large California manufacturers and retailers to disclose their efforts to ensure that slavery is not part of their supply chains, reflects growing awareness and intolerance of the issue. A massive change in the tide took place in December 2011 when Google announced $11.5 million in grants to organizations—including International Justice Mission, a group that rescues girls from sex slavery in India—working to end human trafficking and modern slavery. That message opened eyes around the world.

We are on the eve of the fourth annual Dress for a Good Cause event at its original location. It has expanded to New York, thanks to a motivated high school student. The event's collaborators are joined by supporters as close as a nearby yoga studio that held a fundraiser for projects for survivors, a charming local café that exhibited the Circle of Friends' quilts, and the regional theatre that hosted a panel discussion about human trafficking and slavery. We are grateful to supporters as far away as a high school jewelry club in California that designed beaded and braided bracelets to sell at future Dress events.

Some questions about slavery, child slavery, and sex slavery might never be answered. How can traffickers steal the lives of children? How can a ruthless criminal brutalize another human and still sleep at night? Rather than seeking answers to those mysterious conditions, we can work to put an end to the root causes of slavery and slavery itself.

I never found an answer to the odd question arising from my early dream—*Why were Gandhi and I trying to play basketball?*—and the Indian peacemaker did not revisit in my dreams. My surprise was great, however, when a coordinator at Punarnawa Ashram mentioned that after all other needs were fulfilled, it would be fun for the girls to have a basketball hoop on the campus. I could almost feel his smile at such a possibility.

Appendix—Solutions for Facing and Fighting Child Slavery

I slept and dreamt that life was joy.
I awoke and saw that life was service.
I acted and behold, service was joy.
—Rabindranath Tagore

Problems that seem overwhelming and unsolvable can affect us in three different ways.

1. They can destroy us.
2. We can forget about them. We can push them to hidden depths of our memories where they cannot continue to hurt us.
3. We can use our energy—the powerful force that comes from outrage—to conquer them.

Learning that there are twenty-seven million slaves worldwide today, as estimated by Kevin Bales, cofounder of Free the Slaves, can feel shocking, overwhelming, and insurmountable to some people. The reality that slavery wasn't actually abolished after the US Civil War is disillusioning. That slavery is illegal but covertly persistent in every country in the world—including the United States—is disheartening at minimum. That millions of slaves are children and all too many are victims of sexual exploitation is wrenching.

But this is not an unsolvable problem! People can and are fighting these terrible acts with small- and large-scale solutions. Everyone can help.

Four areas are currently the targets for positive action:

- raising awareness that slavery exists;
- prosecution of traffickers, holders, and abusers;
- support for survivors;
- prevention of slavery.

Within the areas of raising awareness, survivor support, and prevention are many ways mainstream Americans and people in developed nations—teens, moms, concerned citizens, churches, civic organizations, and informal neighborhood groups—can lend a hand. It doesn't take being a millionaire or leaving your state to make a significant difference.

Raising awareness that slavery exists. Many people I meet at the end of speeches or presentations tell me that they didn't know slavery still exists or that it prevails in the United States. The expression "treated like a slave" is sometimes used glibly to imply poor working conditions or low pay; people sometimes confuse sweatshop or poorly paid labor with slavery. Slaves are people who are forced to work without pay by violence or threat of violence to themselves or their loved ones. They cannot leave.

When one person tells another and word of the issue spreads to all corners of our country, there will be fewer places for slavery to hide. Like the exhibit of survivor-made quilts at the Three Little Pigs Café in my town, there are numerous creative vehicles for educating the public.

Supporting survivors. As much as many conscience-driven Westerners would like to, we cannot personally physically help with rescues. In lands where a foreigner with different skin, clothing, language, and customs poking around signals possible detection, holders become yet more stealthy. They recede further into shadows and move slaves to other hidden locations.

Once we are aware of the existence of slavery, however, we can remain alert to situations that don't seem on the up-and-up. For example, Margaret, a truck driver who lives in my county, keeps a magnet with the trafficking hotline number (currently 888-3737-888) on her dashboard. In the event she sees something or someone who seems out of place at a truck stop, she can report what she witnessed.

We can serve as advocates for communities taking their own first steps toward resisting traffickers and slavery, or to demand freedom from current slaveholders. Spreading the word of human atrocities, or governments or people who ignore slaves facing retaliation when working to achieve their freedom, can keep issues from being swept under a rug. Financial donations—to nonprofit organizations that support field workers who fortify communities working for their own liberation—send a strong signal to the striving communities and their criminal oppressors.

We can also help by providing resources for survivors who have been rescued. We can support the schools where survivors can heal and learn. Even small donations can help fund highly specialized medical and psychological treatment, and sow the seeds for sustainable programs and places, such as the bio-gas system and cows at Punarnawa. Survivors take new skills and strength back to their homes and make their villages less susceptible to traffickers' deceit and control.

Furthermore, providing resources to help former slaves might solve slavery better than we could guess. Like Frederick Douglass, an escaped slave in the 1800s who worked tirelessly to free those still held, and Jaya, a rescued survivor who recognized her captor and sought help to save a girl in peril, survivors are likely to know exactly how, under what conditions, and where a human is likely to be taken. When afforded the proper support, they can testify against the perpetrators, keep an eye open for trouble, and report it, helping educate people who were once as vulnerable as they had been.

Prevention. Wiping out root causes of slavery helps prevent further victims. Providing the means for Free the Slaves' workers to educate and help community vigilance committees in particularly vulnerable areas is one way to help. Working on projects toward reading and education, job training, feeding people who may be temporarily down and out on their luck, and that help victims of war-torn areas or natural disasters is like inoculating communities against slavery.

A Few Words on What Doesn't Work

A general boycott of products that might be made with slave labor can actually harm rather than help. For example, if people stop consuming coffee or chocolate altogether, it can put legal, ethical workers out of jobs, creating a larger pool of people who are vulnerable to harm.

Supporting an organization that buys slaves for the purpose of rescuing them, however noble in intention, is supporting an illegal activity and will create more victims. When one child slave is purchased, a criminal will replace him or her with another victim. The more money traffickers and slaveholders control, the stronger they become.

Eighteen Action Items

The following list of action items is compiled from solutions posed by several experts in the field: Kevin Bales, cofounder of Free the Slaves and several of his colleagues; Mark E. Rodgers, dean of the Graduate School of Social Work at Dominican University; various staff members at the Polaris Project; and Ron Chance, a former director of intelligence analysis for the US Department of Labor. It also includes adaptations and solutions of my own.

Raise awareness.

1. Start a conversation among friends, within your church, mosque, temple, meetings, civic groups, clubs, or professional organizations. Raise awareness of the growing demand for child pornography, children in the sex industry, and the increasing use of the Internet for such illegal activity. Demand an end to it.
2. Ask for a presentation or speech. Visit www. facingthemonster.com. Seek out seminars about human trafficking at local universities, churches, the Salvation Army, and other venues.
3. Determine how many slaves could be making your life easy by visiting http://slaveryfootprint.org. Pay close attention to the facts they include on survey pages. You

might learn something about the makeup you wear, the shrimp you eat, and the cell phone you use every day.

4. Find out where there is a museum exhibit on modern slavery. Visit! There's a National Underground Railroad Freedom Center in Cincinnati, Ohio; a traveling museum that highlights slavery in Florida; and the International Slavery Museum in Liverpool, UK, that includes exhibits about historical and contemporary slavery. Or take a trip to a fair-trade town—Media, Pennsylvania; Garstang, UK; or New Koforidua, Ghana.

5. Share this book or the others mentioned with your book club, or donate a copy to your library or a school. *Sold* by Patricia McCormick; *Ending Slavery: How We Free Today's Slaves* by Kevin Bale; and *A Crime So Monstrous* by Ben Skinner are just three additional examples of well-written books on the subject. In *Contemporary Slavery: Teachers' Resource*, teachers can also find lesson plans and materials for students ages ten to fourteen at http://www.liverpoolmuseums.org.uk/ism/learning/slavery-today/.

6. Hang a poster, post a note on Facebook, or tweet a message on Twitter about National Human Trafficking Awareness Day each January 11, as passed by the Senate in 2007. Better yet, make every day an awareness day through social media.

7. Join an established group of abolitionists: Rotarians in an action group; Quakers in a working group; a Free the Slaves' university chapter; or another group in your region. Grassroots organizations are springing up in many towns. If you can't find a group, start one, or become a participant of an online group.

    a. Share information by e-mail or electronic newsletter.

    b. Join forces to make a donation to a survivors' center.

    c. Share news about where to buy fair-trade products.

    d. Write to businesses to ask how they are ensuring that their supply chains are not based on slave labor.

8. Learn signs of human trafficking and what to do if you suspect it. The Polaris Project's website offers information especially for medical professionals, educators, and law enforcement officers: http://www.polarisproject. org/resources/tools-for-service-providers-and-law-enforcement.

9. Change your thinking. Is the young woman you saw in the city or at your hotel when you traveled to the Super Bowl (the top American football game in the United States) or another major sports event elsewhere really a partying prostitute who wants to trade sex for money? Or is she a victim who is being coerced to pretend she likes her work in order to stay alive? According to a January 30, 2011, *Newsweek* article, "The big game's dark side" is a "surge in human trafficking ..."

Provide support for survivors.

10. Make a donation to a nonprofit organization that has expertise and experience helping survivors: Free the Slaves, Dawn's Place, International Justice Mission, Anti-Slavery International in the UK, your local crime victims' center, and many others in the US and elsewhere. Check that an organization is credible and doing what they claim to do with donations; then contribute!

11. Donate gently worn dresses and jewelry to the event Dress for a Good Cause (visit http://www.dressforagoodcause. com/ for more information). Hold your own Dress fundraiser and donate proceeds to antitrafficking organizations. Come up with another way to raise funds— ask a local restaurant or café to donate a percentage of the day's profits in return for publicizing their establishment and sending patrons on a given day.

12. Find out what's happening in the area of legislation for your geographic region. Free the Slaves' and Polaris Project's websites are good places to start to look for information. Let your elected officials know that human trafficking is intolerable.

Help prevent slavery.

13. Buy fair-trade products. Carefully consider what you are buying—if the price seems "too good to be true," it might be. The certifications are numerous to keep track of—Fair Trade, Direct Trade, and others—but they all aim for the same thing. They try to ensure that people are not exploited in the making of the product. For an overview, visit: http://www.firstfairtradetownusa.org/ fair-trade.

14. Fight the root causes of slavery by assisting with local and global projects. By eliminating illiteracy, poverty, and hunger, you are thwarting slavery.
    a. Help teach children or immigrants to read.
    b. Support agencies that teach job skills to people who are unemployed or underemployed—many people really would prefer a "hand up" for self-sufficiency, not a "hand out" of charity.

    c. Make sure a recipient is a reliable agency, nonprofit organization, or volunteer group, and then determine how you can lend a hand.

    d. Donate your dollars, talents, time, or service to a Rotary project or another civic organization's endeavor.

15. Invest with social responsibility.

16. Write to corporations for whom you are a customer or shareholder. Ask how they are working to ensure that slave labor is not part of their supply chain.

17. Lead or join a project to improve educational and awareness programs in schools and thereby reduce children's risk of becoming victims of human trafficking/slavery. Develop relationships with the local Salvation Army, local law enforcement, and other organizations that conduct programs to help victims and alert communities to local dangers.

18. Build a relationship with a child or teen who could be at risk for harm. Volunteer at a youth center or for a children's community art program. The care you show might be the reason kids stay in school, decide not to run away from home, or don't end up in a vulnerable position.

According to UNICEF, as many as two million children are subjected to commercial sexual exploitation in the global commercial sex trade. Please choose to work to make a change. The previously mentioned eighteen easy, concrete ways to help don't require leaving the borders of your town or spending a fortune. These are just a few solutions; there are probably infinite ways to help eradicate slavery.

The fight to end slavery will take cooperation and commitment from people of all walks of life, all neighborhoods and lands, all faiths, and all political backgrounds. It will take people with a range of talents and skills. There is room for your creativity, your unique way of solving problems, and your special gifts.

In the words of Robert Schuller, as painted on the dormitory wall at Punarnawa Ashram, "What would you attempt to do if you knew you could not fail?"

Sources

Bales, Kevin. *Disposable People: New Slavery in the Global Economy.* Revised ed. 1999. Reprint, Los Angeles: University of California Press, 2004.

_____. *Ending Slavery: How We Free Today's Slaves.* Los Angeles: University of California Press, 2007.

Bales, Kevin, and Ron Soodalter. *The Slave Next Door: Human Trafficking and Slavery in America Today.* Los Angeles: University of California Press, 2009.

Batstone, David. *Not For Sale: The Return of the Global Slave Trade and How We Can Fight It.* San Francisco: HyperionSanFrancisco, 2007.

Chance, Ron. Telephone interview by author, October 18, 2010.

Free the Slaves. Last modified 2012. http://www.freetheslaves.net.

Goldberg, Michelle. "The Super Bowl of Sex Trafficking." *The Daily Beast/Newsweek*, January 30, 2011. http://www.

thedailybeast.com/newsweek/2011/01/30/the-super-bowl-of-sex-trafficking.html.

International Justice Mission. Last modified 2012. http://www.ijm.org.

Kristof, Nicholas D. "The Face of Modern Slavery." *The New York Times/The Opinion Pages*, November 16, 2011. http://www.nytimes.com/2011/11/17/opinion/kristof-the-face-of-modern-slavery.html.

McCormick, Patricia. *Sold*. 2008 ed., 2006. Reprint, New York: First Hyperion Paperbacks, 2008.

Polaris Project. Polaris Project: "Combating Human Trafficking and Modern-Day Slavery." Last modified 2010. http://www.polarisproject.org.

Rodgers, Mark E. "The Campaign to Rescue and Restore Victims of Human Trafficking." Lecture, Sykes Auditorium, West Chester University, March 16, 2011.

Salvation Army. "Combating Human Trafficking." Accessed April 19, 2012. http://www.salvationarmyusa.org/usn/www_usn_2.nsf/0/8081A4079639D55A802573E000530965?openDocument.

Skinner, E. Benjamin. *A Crime So Monstrous: Face-to-Face with Modern-Day Slavery*. New York: Free Press, 2008.

Slavery Footprint—Made in a Free World. Accessed April 19, 2012. http://slaveryfootprint.org.

Truckers Against Trafficking. Last modified 2012. http://www.truckersagainsttrafficking.com.

About the Author

Carol Hart Metzker is a writer, frequent speaker, and coauthor of the book *Appreciative Intelligence: Seeing the Mighty Oak in the Acorn* (now in five languages, listed on *Harvard Business Review*'s 2006 list of recommended reading). She has twenty years' experience in communications and project leadership for local and international initiatives. Her articles about innovation, corporate social responsibility, and community development have appeared in numerous international publications. Her projects in India, Ghana (Africa), and Honduras have served as subjects for articles and speeches to groups from the United States to Australia. In May 2010 Carol received a Service Above Self award, Rotary International's highest award for an individual's humanitarian service.

Writing assignments about large companies and information technology have led her to India, where in 2004 she met an eleven-year-old girl rescued from slavery. The encounter led to her journey into the dark world of human trafficking, forced sex trade, and child slavery locally and overseas. It sparked her quest and subsequent projects to aid survivors of modern slavery.

Carol earned a master's degree from George Mason University. She and her husband, residents of West Chester, Pennsylvania, and their two adult daughters work together on projects to aid survivors of slavery and human trafficking.

Let's Face the Monster Together!

Invite Carol Hart Metzker to your next meeting or conference and begin to address the issue of modern slavery.

Carol delivers truths about child slavery and solutions to the problem in sensitive, compelling, and inspiring presentations and interactive sessions. For more information, visit www.facingthemonster.com or e-mail echmetzker@aol.com.

Open Book Editions
A Berrett-Koehler Partner

Open Book Editions is a joint venture between Berrett-Koehler Publishers and Author Solutions, the market leader in self-publishing. There are many more aspiring authors who share Berrett-Koehler's mission than we can sustainably publish. To serve these authors, Open Book Editions offers a comprehensive self-publishing opportunity.

A Shared Mission

Open Book Editions welcomes authors who share the Berrett-Koehler mission—Creating a World That Works for All. We believe that to truly create a better world, action is needed at all levels—individual, organizational, and societal. At the individual level, our publications help people align their lives with their values and with their aspirations for a better world. At the organizational level, we promote progressive leadership and management practices, socially responsible approaches to business, and humane and effective organizations. At the societal level, we publish content that advances social and economic justice, shared prosperity, sustainability, and new solutions to national and global issues.

Open Book Editions represents a new way to further the BK mission and expand our community. . We look forward to helping more authors challenge conventional thinking, introduce new ideas, and foster positive change.

For more information, see the Open Book Editions website: http://www.iuniverse.com/Packages/OpenBookEditions.aspx

Join the BK Community! See exclusive author videos, join discussion groups, find out about upcoming events, read author blogs, and much more! http://bkcommunity.com/

Made in the USA
Lexington, KY
09 September 2013